AF600493

THE CATHOLIC UNIVERSITY OF AMERICA
CANON LAW STUDIES
Number 88

PARISH REGISTERS

AN HISTORICAL SYNOPSIS AND COMMENTARY

A DISSERTATION

Submitted to the Faculty of Canon Law of the Catholic University of America in Partial Fulfillment of the Requirements for the Degree of

DOCTOR OF CANON LAW

BY

REV. JAMES J. O'ROURKE, A.B., J.C.L.,
Priest of the Archdiocese of Philadelphia

THE CATHOLIC UNIVERSITY OF AMERICA
WASHINGTON, D. C.
1934

Nihil Obstat:

VALENTINUS SCHAAF, O.F.M., J.C.D.,
Censor Deputatus.

Washingtonii, D. C., die XXI Aprilis, 1934.

Imprimatur:

DIONYSIUS CARDINALIS DOUGHERTY,
Archiepiscopus Philadelphiensis.

Philadelphiae, die XXVIII, Aprilis, 1934.

Printed by
THE PAULIST PRESS
New York, N. Y.

TO MY MOTHER

TABLE OF CONTENTS

FOREWORD

THE writer takes this occasion to offer his sincere thanks to all those who aided him to carry on and complete this work. To those who assisted more than they are aware with their generosity and encouragement of various kinds the author gives here an assurance of a continued gratefulness. More particularly the writer wishes to express his deep appreciation of the aid given him by the Faculty of the Graduate School of Canon Law, The Reverend Doctors Schaaf, Motry, Roelker, Lardone and Mr. Fox, whose direction and advice have done so much toward making the publication of this monograph possible and finally, to the Rev. F. X. Wahl for assistance in reading the proofs.

INTRODUCTION

AMONG the phases of the life of the Church which Canon Law regulates, the sacramental system occupies a prominent place. Naturally this should be so since it is through the agency of the Sacraments that grace, the means of sanctification and salvation for the members of this society, is in great part provided.[1] Such being the case, the Code of Canon Law, concerned as it is chiefly with the Church as an external society, gives a thorough consideration to the sacramental system at least in so far as it affects the exterior order. Hence the Canons on the administration and reception of the Sacraments are large in number and usually rather detailed in regulation.

From the canonical point of view all of the Sacraments are important, of course, but Baptism and Matrimony may be said to assume a peculiar importance. The former because of its characteristic effect upon a person with regard to the society of the Church [2] and the latter on account of its many and various ramifications.

Without baptism membership in the society of Christ is impossible. Citizenship in the Church has its origin in the reception of this Sacrament [3] and upon this indispensable initiation all future activities in the Church depend.[4] As for Matrimony, the laws prescribing and regulating the use of the canonical form of themselves suffice to render it of outstanding importance in the field of Canon Law.

As has been said above canonical regulations on the Sacraments are often very thorough and the subject of this dissertation deals with some such detailed regulations. Through Baptism man acquires the status of a person with rights and duties in the Church.[5] At times it may be necessary to prove the possession of this juridical personality, hence the Code of Canon Law demands the drawing and

[1] Canon 731, § 1.

[2] John iii, 5; Tanquerey, *Synopsis Theologiae Dogmaticae,* I, 386.

[3] Canon 87.

[4] Canon 737.

[5] Canon 87.

keeping of such proving documents or records.[6] In marriage as well documents of proof must be had concerning the observance of the laws of the Church in this matter.[7]

In one general Canon,[8] therefore, the Code of Canon Law requires the pastor to draw and maintain such records, called therein parochial books. Besides records of the baptism and marriages in his parish he must have records of confirmations, deaths and the *status animarum*. This last is a less determined register which deals, as far as possible, with the more general spiritual status of the individual members of the parish during the more ordinary periods of life.

It is under the title Parish Registers that these official records,[9] called in the Code of Canon Law parochial books, are to be treated. As has been stated above only those five books explicitly named in Canon 470, the books of the baptized and the confirmed, the matrimonial register, the book wherein the deceased are recorded and finally that known as the *status animarum* are included. Books concerning the financial matters of the parish, registers of Masses, etc., find no place in this work.

The first part of this dissertation confines itself to the fundamental notions and the second to the history of the subject. The latter is brief since the lack of sources and the peculiar development of legislation on the parochial books preclude a fuller study. Nevertheless it is hoped that the historical treatment will be extensive enough to serve its chief purpose, a background for the commentary which will constitute the third and concluding portion of this work. Present day legislation in no small part is derived from that of pre-Code times, hence the value of the historical section is quite obvious.

[6] Canon 777.

[7] Canons 1103, 1107.

[8] Canon 470: A measure strengthened and enlarged upon by many other Canons in the third book of the Code.

[9] Canon 1813, § 1, 4°.

PART I

PRELIMINARY DISCUSSION

CHAPTER I

FUNDAMENTAL NOTIONS

THE practical application of the law on parish registers necessarily involves the treatment of several diverse but mutually complementary subjects. Canon 470 not only prescribes the maintenance of the five books mentioned therein, the contents of which are regulated elsewhere [1] but also embodies other regulations, (use of parochial archive, seal, for example) calculated to secure a detailed accomplishment of the purpose of the legislation. There are, too, general regulations applicable to all the parochial records to be considered which render the arrangement of such matters difficult. Hence the purpose here will be to treat of the fundamental notions, including such required adjuncts as mentioned above, and the general relations of the pastor to the registers, so that the later commentary may concern itself wholly with the contents of the books, thereby avoiding any repetition.

ARTICLE I

THE NATURE OF THE REGISTERS IN CANON LAW

The primary purpose motivating legislation on the parish registers is the matter of proof. Both the records themselves and the certificates drawn therefrom are public ecclesiastical documents.[2] As such they have full value as proof concerning those things directly and principally set forth in their contents.[3] Their public nature arises from the fact that they are made by a person constituted and acting as a public official,[4] and in a form determined by law.[5] The eccle-

[1] Canons 777, 798, 1103, 1238, 1011, 576, § 2.

[2] Canons 1813, 1814.

[3] Canon 1816.

[4] Vermeersch-Creusen, *Epitome,* III, p. 77; Blat declares the pastor to be a notary, however it appears that this is subject to qualification. The Sacred

siastical nature of the same records is obvious enough since they contain evidence of the performance of certain ecclesiastical functions.[6] Hence it is apparent that the precise status of the members of the society of the Church can be demonstrated by the use of these authentic records. They give evidence concerning the administration of the Sacraments and trace the advancement of the members through the various stages of progress possible in the Church.[7]

Article II

General Relations of the Pastor and Parish Registers

Complete control of the parochial records is in the hands of the pastor.[8] The various rights and duties that constitute this pastoral control over the parochial records will be seen throughout the commentary each in its proper place. There are, however, a few exceptions to this exercise of complete control by the pastor. First, the Ordinary of the place is the inspector of these books and during his visitation of the parish this should be one of the matters attended to.[9]

Congregation of the Council decided that the pastor is had as a notary when he is inscribing in his books or drawing certificates from his own parochial registers but not in other cases, *e.g.*, were he to attempt the recording of a baptism in his register from a certificate given elsewhere. Blat, *Commentarium*, III, p. 655; S. C. C., July 3, 1909, n. I—*A. A. S.*, I (1909), 658.

[5] Canons 470, 777, 798, etc.

[6] Vermeersch-Creusen, *Epitome*, III, 78.

[7] Blat, *De Personis*, p. 506.

Civil Law Status: If the register entries are kept in the way to be suggested herein they will constitute admissible evidence under the rules of evidence in force in common law jurisdictions in the United States of America. They will evidence facts recorded therein of the officiating clergyman's personal knowledge. If the entry be composite (drawn by a minister other than the pastor and then subsigned by the pastor) again they evidence facts of the officiating clergyman's personal knowledge. For example: the baptismal record will evidence that the living child was baptized on such a date but will not evidence the date of birth.

For other countries the civil law of such places will have to be consulted. The Napoleonic Code and concordats with the Holy See will probably play some part in determining the civil status of parish registers in some countries.

[8] Wernz-Vidal, *Jus Canonicum*, II, p. 796.

[9] Canon 470, § 4: Any other opportune time will be equally acceptable.

After the inspection it would be well for the Ordinary to inscribe the registers to the effect that he has seen them, with his signature and the date.

The second exception takes the form of the canonical regulation [10] which requires the annual forwarding of exemplars of all the registrations made in the parochial books during the year. These are to be sent by the respective pastors to the episcopal curia of the diocese. The same Canon, however, expressly excuses the pastors from giving a report on the book of the *status animarum* since the purpose for which this register was instituted renders it of no value save in the proper parish.[11]

The reason behind the prescription of the annual report is one of caution. It is a preventive measure placed against such confusion as would arise from the destruction of the parish records by fire or other means as happened in many countries during the World War.[12] This yearly copy is to be an authentic one hence signed by the pastor himself and impressed with the parish seal [13] though the actual drawing up of such a copy may be left in the hands of another.[14]

Authors fail to say what this report should contain but it is evident that if the purpose of the law is to be fulfilled then the chancery archives must be able to supply the documentary evidence that would otherwise be completely lost with the destruction of the original parochial records. Therefore, these various exemplars must be complete and exact facsimiles of the records for the year. Practically, for the chancery to be able to conserve these annual reports a large archive will have to be maintained and in such a way that each parish will be given a particular and commodious file for its reports.

The Code prescribes that these registers be parochial books, that is, a collection of books, not loose papers or certificates, and dedicated to the sole purpose of registering the official ecclesiastical acts from

[10] Canon 470, § 3; Cocchi, *Commentarium,* II, I, II, 411.

[11] Blat, *Commentarium,* II, 505.

[12] Chelodi, *De Personis,* n. 228 (note 1 on p. 380).

[13] Vermeersch-Creusen, *Epitome,* I, 325; Blat, *Commentarium,* II, 506.

[14] Gasparri, *De Matrimonio,* II, p. 256; Wernz-Vidal, *De Matrimonio,* p. 665; Blat, *Commentarium,* II, 596.

which each one draws its name [15] in accordance with the prescriptions of the Roman Ritual and the Code. The books should be of good quality linen paper, well-bound in view of the length of service they are to see as reference books and an ample index will facilitate their use as such.[16] Loose-leaf volumes are of no use since their employment entails the possibility of fraudulent practise. One page or many could be removed and the mutilation easily pass undetected. Even in the well-bound books both the pages and the individual inscription should be numbered, the latter serialized by the year.

Some authors have given consideration to the use of the index cards instead of books for the record of the *status animarum*.[17] From a practical point of view this is a very helpful suggestion and well within the bounds of canonical regulation since a great deal of latitude is given in the matter of this register.[18] However, it must be remembered that index cards cannot be utilized for the other four registers.

1. *The Inscription*

Canon 470, § 1 next imposes upon the pastor the duty of making the inscription in these books required by approved use in the Church and by the prescriptions of the Ordinary. Concerning these norms for inscribing Blat [19] admits the following of episcopal direction in things proper to the place [20] but requires adherence to the general regulations of the Roman Ritual in substance and to the Code of Canon Law.[21]

The contents of the inscription have no place here but the means employed to enter such information deserve a little attention. The kind of ink to be used is a worthwhile point for consideration as those who have handled aged registers realize. There are many brands of

15 Sipos, *Enchiridion*, 305; Monacelli, *Formularium Fori Ecclesiastici*, I, X, 2, 286; Gasparri, *De Matrimonio*, n. 1073.

16 Heiner, *De Processu Criminali Eccles.*, p. 30.

17 Vromat, *Jus Missionariorum*, III, 4, 306; Fanfani, *De Jure Parochorum*, p. 71.

18 Canon 470; Sipos, *Enchiridion*, 306; Fanfani, *op. cit.*, p. 71.

19 *Commentarium*, II, 505.

20 Example see Vlaming, *Praelectiones*, p. 211, note.

21 Vromant, *Jus Missionariorum*, II, 296.

writing fluid upon the market today which are guaranteed not to fade as ordinary writing ink is wont to do. One of these should be employed in entering the inscriptions that they may retain their proper value in the future.[22] Care, too, should be taken to write as plainly as possible avoiding cramping and unorthodox abbreviations, paying particular attention to the spelling of all names and places.[23] On the other hand, it should be borne in mind that the inscription is not to assume too large a form thereby preventing any further recording because two of the registers, the baptismal, particularly, and the matrimonial, may need to be annotated at some later date. Formerly the pastor was required to inscribe the records *manu sua* but the Code has not seen fit to include this,[24] his subsignation now suffices.[25]

Concerning the language to be used most authors say nothing. This perhaps may be construed as an argument for the employing of Latin since all their formulae are couched in that tongue. Cappello [26] alone makes any mention of the point declaring that it remains for episcopal prescription, custom of the diocese or synodal law to regulate this matter. Latin should be employed in any case where the matter to be entered might be productive of scandal if able to be read by others than the proper persons. If one is free to use the vernacular in inscribing it might be well to employ it since the possibility of mistakes will thereby be lessened. Also the fact that the certificates are ordinarily drawn in that tongue counsels the use of the same in the register. If the certificate is to be transmitted to a foreign country a translation into Latin can be made.

The final point to be made with regard to the inscription deals with the matter of correcting the contents of a given book. Sipos [27] and Cappello [28] are of the opinion that no corrections are to be made without the permission of the Ordinary and if such is secured then note of it is to be made in the record thus corrected. A better

[22] Heiner, *op cit.*, p. 30.

[23] *"Sedulo"* says Canon 777, § 1; Augustine, *A Commentary,* IV, 95.

[24] Cappello, *De Sacramentis,* III, 767-768.

[25] Vermeersch-Creusen, *Epitome,* II, 28.

[26] *De Sacramentis,* I, 142, 139.

[27] *Enchiridion,* p. 264.

[28] *De Sacramentis,* I, 192.

way would be to place the correction in the form of a note in the column reserved for remarks. The reason for thus handling a correction is that unless some such means is taken to safeguard it the authenticity of said record might be easily attacked. The best way to forestall any attempt to attack the registration is to forego all manner of erasures, cancellations, etc., and impose an entirely new record, elsewhere if necessary, connecting the old and the new entry with cross-references.

The above named authors, however, when demanding the permission of the Ordinary for a pastor to correct a record, are dealing with a condition peculiar to some European countries. In these places the civil law gives recognition to the parochial records but demands the fulfillment of some specific civil regulations in their regard. One of these makes it incumbent upon the Bishop to supervise all corrections of the registers. In our country this condition does not exist hence the pastor by virtue of his office is able to make the necessary corrections without any reference to the Ordinary. Because of this he should take special care that he safeguard his corrections, either by giving notice of them in the column of remarks or by using the method of the new entry with cross-references. The matter of fraudulent alterations, corrections, etc., will be dealt with when consideration is given the penalties to be inflicted for the neglect of the pastoral duty toward the parochial books.

2. *Custody of the Registers*

Since these are books containing information of a private nature and are necessary for reference they must be guarded accordingly. The Code therefore cautions the pastor to be diligent in this matter [29] and to insure a proper custody requires their keeping in a parochial archive [30] that the records may not be lost or become mutilated.[31] This archive need not be a pretentious affair and the sacristy or rectory safe may well be used as the place of maintenance. Generally speaking, the place where the *res sacra* are stored will be

[29] Canons 470, § 1; 2382.
[30] Canon 470, § 4.
[31] Sipos, *Enchiridion*, p. 306.

sufficient [32] under lock and key however.[33] The same rules as apply to diocesan archives with the necessary modifications are to be enforced here.[34] The original documents can be removed only with permission and then for three days' time only.[35] Circumstances may warrant its prolongation moderately [36] and in all cases a signed notice indicating the removal of the registers must be left with the one in charge. Finally it must be remembered that documents of a non-secret nature may be seen by those who have a legitimate interest in them and they have a right to a copy of such a document [37] when they conform with the rules laid down by those in authority.[38] The nature of the parish records requires that the person who will handle these books should be one in whom some official authority has been placed. Some authors are of the opinion that it is not a laudable practise to allow sacristans to keep these records.[39] The Code itself cautions the pastor to be careful lest the records come into the hands of extraneous persons. This caution precludes the practise of allowing them to lay about the rectory or elsewhere in open view where domestics and other persons may have ready access to them.[40]

3. *Certificates*

The Code speaks of certificates as authentic documents [41] and declares them to be of probative value equal to that of the registers themselves. To meet the requirements of that Canon these *partitae* must be signed by the pastor and ought to be fortified with the impression of the parish seal. In this manner they are rendered authentic and complete.[42] On the question of what is to be tran-

[32] Gasparri, *De Matrimonio* (3rd edition), II, 256.

[33] Wernz-Vidal, *Jus Canonicum,* II, 794.

[34] Canons 378, 381, § 1, 384.

[35] Canons 378, § 1; 383.

[36] Canon 378, § 1.

[37] Canon 384, § 1.

[38] Canon 384, § 2.

[39] Gasparri, *De Matrimonio,* II, p. 254, (3rd edition); Vromant, *Jus Missionariorum,* III, 308.

[40] Augustine, *A Commentary,* II, 555.

[41] Canon 1813, § 1, 4°; Fanfani, *De Jure Parochorum,* p. 243.

[42] Capello, *De Sacramentis,* I, p. 140.

scribed from the content of the register to the certificate some authors [43] demand that it be *de verbo ad verbum*. Cappello [44] denies this no matter what may be the desired use for the certificate. In ordinary cases so long as the authenticity of the certificate can be recognized from the pastor's signature and the parochial seal, and the necessary information contained therein [45] nothing further is required. Here it may be added that if a certificate is desired merely to demonstrate baptism without any relation to the contracting of marriage, it will not be necessary to include the annotations that may be found in the baptismal record, though some advise the giving of the entire content every time.[46] Finally the vernacular should be used in the drawing up of the certificates as may be easily seen from the use they are destined for. If, however, they are to be transmitted to non-English speaking countries the employment of Latin will be necessary.

The decision of the Sacred Congregation of the Council referred to above settled several matters of importance. It supported the juridical value of the certificates but in particular cases demanded the employment of additional safeguards for their acceptation with full force and credence.[47] In such cases as necessitated the transmission of a certificate from one country to another the Congregation declared that the document should be fortified with the signature and the seal of the Ordinary of the place whence the document came. Also, the recognition of such a document as authentic belongs not to the pastor but to the Ordinary of the place to which it is transmitted.[48]

A distinction is made concerning the pastor's status when he is drawing a certificate from his parochial books and when he is inscribing such registers from a certificate, as has been touched upon previously. In the former case universal custom interprets his acts

[43] Giraldi, *Ad Barbosam,* I, VII, 21, 64; Lucidi, *De Visit. SS. Lim.*, I, 248; Gasparri, *De Matrimonio,* II, 172.

[44] *De Sacramentis,* I, 140.

[45] The register alone can be used as the source of the information; S. C. C., July 3, 1909, n. II—*A. A. S.*, I (1909), 657-660.

[46] *Il Monitore Ecclesiastico,* XXX (1918), 219.

[47] *A. A. S.*, I (1909), 660.

[48] *Op. cit.*, pp. 658, 660.

as those of a public ecclesiastical notary and as such the instruments that he draws from his records have the juridical value of the original records. In the latter case, which is the matter principally set before the Congregation here, his pastoral office of itself does not suffice to make such a registration authentic. Either the bishop should constitute him as a notary to perform such an inscription or have the chancellor or another already constituted ecclesiastical notary authenticate the inscription. Finally, if the bishop authorizes the pastor to enter the inscription in his parochial register the certificate is to be kept not in the parochial archives but in those of the bishop.

Generally speaking what control does the bishop exercise over these documents? Must the certificate in every case have the episcopal recognition when it is to be sent out of the diocese? Not necessarily, unless there is a diocesan law to that effect,[49] but in view of the decision of the Sacred Congregation of the Council given above it would certainly expedite matters if in all cases of extra-diocesan transmission this procedure was followed. In some dioceses particular law demands the curial recognition even for intra-diocesan transmission.[50] Such a law however cannot strike at the authenticity of the certificate and anyone acting contrary to such a prescription would in no wise impugn the validity of the document since common law includes no such regulation for authentic inscription. The same would be true even if the Ordinary placed such a condition under pain of nullity of the certification.

4. *The Parochial Seal*

Besides the affixing of the pastor's signature to the certificate, it is to be impressed with the parish seal. This is a mark in corroboration of its authenticity, making the document complete.[51] The pastor has the right and the duty to have such a seal because he is a witness qualified in those things pertaining to his office.[52] Beyond

[49] Cappello, *De Sacramentis,* I, 140.
[50] Cappello, *De Sacramentis,* I. 140.
[51] De Meester, *Juris Canonici,* II, VII, 322.
[52] Wernz-Vidal, *Jus Canonicum,* II, 795.

this there is little to be said concerning this official instrument. All are more or less acquanted with this seal, either the paper crushing one or the rubber stamp kind. There is little to choose between them though the former kind is reputed to be more safe from tampering.

The final point to be treated in this matter of the certificates is that of the fee. Rather conflicting opinions have been held from time to time. Baruffaldus [53] said that some fee could be expected by the pastor in consideration of the labor and the expense entailed. Barbosa [54] declared that custom was to be followed in this matter. Cappello [55] with a distinction clearly defines the point at issue. A proportionate fee may be sought or demanded if legitimate custom warrants it or if a regulation rightly in accord with Canons 1507 and 463 permits. If however neither of these support the action the fee cannot be exacted. As is usual in all such matters, such services are to be offered the poor *gratis*.

5. *Penalties*

The penal law of the Code [56] visualizes three classes of offense against the canonical regulations concerning the parish registers. The first is verified when the pastor does not maintain the parish records. Neither their inscription nor their proper custody is attended to. In such a case the law allows the Ordinary full power in determining the extent of the penalty to be imposed, however demanding the gravity of the fault to be the guiding norm in the action. The second class deals with such acts as prevent the registers from bearing honest testimony. Canon 2406 expressly imposes privation of office besides the punishment the Ordinary is empowered to inflict. Falsification, the writing of a false document, adulteration, the effecting of a substantial change, destruction and occult sequestration of the registers are the condemned actions.[57] Privation of office or suspension from the same together with a pecuniary fine proportionate to the

[53] *Comment. ad Rit. Roman.*, I, II, 218.

[54] *Giraldi, Ad Barbosam*, I, VII, 19-20, 34.

[55] *De Sacramentis*, I, 143.

[56] Canons 2383, 2406.

[57] Sipos, *Enchiridion*, 264.

offense is the legal sanction for the third class of violation, namely refusal to draw up a document, transmit it or exhibit the registers to one asking the same with a legitimate right. Also any other betrayal of the pastoral trust in this regard merits the same penalty. The refusal however must be a qualified one, entailing a grave deceit.[58] The same author says the general words of the Canon leave it to the Ordinary's prudent judgment to decide whether or not this illegal action should be the cause of inflicting a penalty.

6. *The Subject of This Legislation*

Throughout the foregoing reference has been made solely to the pastor as the one obliged personally and *sub gravi* to maintain the parochial records and to issue the certificates drawn from them.[59] Canon 470 speaks of these obligations as incumbent upon the pastor. What part therefore has the assistant or curate in these affairs? In common law the assistant has no right or duty in this regard.[60] This matter is only a consequent of the question concerning the curateship as a strict ecclesiastical office. The preponderance of opinion seems to favor his having only delegated powers [61] and De Meester [62] explicitly declares that it belongs to the pastor to make the inscriptions in the records and to issue certificates. He adds however that the care of such matters is usually handed over to the curate.

With regard to the registration of marriage a difference is had which will be treated in the proper place. Here and now it is a question of the assistant's relations to the registers in general. The pastor, including those whom the common law endows with the parochial powers, (quasi-pastor, econome and substitute pastor unless expressly restricted),[63] alone is empowered with the rights and duties of registration and the curate, therefore, is totally incapable of any such performance. However, the determination of the assistant's

[58] Vermeersch-Creusen, *Epitome,* III, n. 612.

[59] Cappello, *De Sacramentis,* I, n. 188.

[60] Augustine, *A Commentary,* VII, 257; Chelodi, *De Personis,* n. 232.

[61] Bastnagel, *Appointment of Adjutors and Assistants,* p. 144. See this dissertation for a thorough treatment of the whole subject.

[62] *Juris Canonici,* II, VII, n. 887.

[63] Canons 471-475.

rights and duties is left in the hands of the diocesan statutes, the letters of assignment by the Ordinary and the pastor's commission. Hence any difficulties from the practical point of view may be easily removed by these agencies. Finally, De Meester [64] declares that these acts belong to the secondary class of parochial functions and allows the curate to presume the pastor's permission when the provisions of Canon 476, § 6 have not been sufficiently utilized to care for a given situation.

[64] *Juris Canonici*, II, VII, n. 892.

PART II

HISTORICAL SYNOPSIS

CHAPTER II

PARISH REGISTERS BEFORE THE COUNCIL OF TRENT

ARTICLE I

THE PARISH—PASTOR SITUATION

SINCE these registers are inextricably associated with the parish today, it is of importance to consider, though briefly, the parish and the pastor during the earliest period of Christianity.

Parishes did not always have a place in the ecclesiastical organization and pastors, as such, were unknown at one time. The marked silence of the more ancient sources has led the generality of authorities to assert the non-existence of parishes throughout the first three centuries, at least.[1] The parish was coextensive with the diocese, the very name was so applied,[2] and the faithful depended directly upon the bishop for ministrations.[3]

The recognition of Christianity effected a tremendous change. To meet conditions attendant upon numerous conversions it was necessary to erect new churches and to apportion to priests duties that formerly devolved on the bishop alone. In the country districts it would seem such churches became of some parochial standing about the fourth century.[4] In the cities, some time passed before they acquired the status of parish churches, in the true sense. Their dependence upon the episcopal church continued and the clergy attached to the bishop, carried on such functions as were to be per-

[1] Thomassin, *Vet. et Nov. Eccl. Discipl.* Pars I, lib. II, cap. XXI, Parg. 1-4; Devoti, *Inst. Canon.*, Lib. II, tit. III, sect. X, LXXXVII; Wernz, *Jus Decretalium*, II, Parg. 84, III; Smith, *Elements of Ecclesiastical Law*, n. 639, 2.

[2] Rossi, *De Paroecia*, p. 3.

[3] *Prompta Bibliotheca*, "parochia," n. 7; Rossi, De Paroecia, pp. 8, 9.

[4] Devoti, *Inst. Canon.*, I, tit. III, sect. X, LXXXIX; Thomassin, *op. cit.*, I, II, XXII, Parg. 3, 10; Innocent I, *Epist. I ad Decentium*, c. 5, *Mansi* III, 1030; C. Sardicia, c. 6 (347), *Mansi* III, 10; C. Chalcedon, c. 17 (451), *Mansi* VIII, 397.

formed.[5] These churches were as Rossi [6] says *"quasi ecclesiae matrici subsidiariae."* It was not until about the year 1000 that cities, save great centers like Rome and Alexandria, were divided into parishes.[7] It can be supposed that some time elapsed between the establishment of parishes and the acquiring of a determined status by the one in care of the souls, the pastor. Wernz-Vidal [8] declares the eleventh century saw the widespread division of dioceses into parishes and he maintains that the Council of Trent really gave the pastor his now established place in the organization of the Church.

The development of the parochial registers waited upon the evolution of the parish and the parochial office. Hence in the earliest periods the nonexistence of parochial books depends in great part upon this deficiency; later, the legislation is enacted when the Sacraments are being considered and still later the title "Pastors, their Rights and Duties" comes to embrace laws in this regard as a part of its ambitus.

Article II

Earliest Registers

Here attention is directed to what appears to be the forerunners of the parochial registers, the diptychs. In the diptychs of the baptized and the dead are seen some of the characteristics of the books demanded in legislation of later times but it is doubtful whether the connection between the diptychs and the parochial books is strong enough to stand too much stressing.

1. *The Baptismal Record Up to the Thirteenth Century*

In the very early days of Christianity quasi-baptismal registers were not lacking.[9] The newly-baptized were recorded on what were

[5] Bingham, *The Antiquities of the Christian Church,* IX, VIII, VI.

[6] *De Paroecia,* p. 11.

[7] Bouix, *De Parocho,* I, III, 1; Devoti, *Inst. Canon.,* I, III, X, LXXXVII, note 1.

[8] *De Personis,* p. 774.

[9] Saegmüller, Die Kirchenbücher in Kath. Deutschland, *T. Q. S.,* LXXXI (1899), p. 216 sq.

known as the diptychs of the baptized. The diptych, as the name suggests, a folded parchment giving the appearance of a two page book, was carried over from the Roman civil document to do service in the Church.[10] This tablet was a kind of a baptismal register [11] in which the names of the recently baptized and those of the parents were inscribed.[12] These were not read as was usually the case of diptychs but were preserved in the bishop's house because the bishop had full contact with the faithful as pastor and by means of these diptychs the people were numbered and known.[13]

Many of the Fathers of the Church bear witness to the existence of this quasi-baptismal register but the similarity ought not be overstressed [14] because of the indefiniteness of the excerpts.[15]

The diptych continued to be used for a considerable period, but the startling effect upon the fortunes of the Christian religion produced by Constantine's edict of Milan (311 A. D.) and the consequent establishment of that religion in the Empire made the baptismal diptych dwindle in importance until "these records (the various kinds of diptychs) were lost in the course of time because when Christianity became the State religion the civil registers took their places." [16] Hence as far as the sources attainable are concerned all through the period of the union of the Church and State, the baptismal register as a public record demanded today by ecclesiastical legislation seems to have had no existence and even up to the thirteenth century it is lacking.

[10] Cabrol, "Diptychon," *Dict. Lit. et d'Arch Chret.*, IV, I, 1040, d.

[11] *Cath. Encycl.*, art. Register, V, 23.

[12] Smith & Cheetham, *Dictionary of Christian Antiquities*, p. 561.

[13] Selvagio, *Inst. Antiq. Christ*, IV, III, II, p. 84; Catalanus, *Rit. Roman. Benedict XIV*, I, 32; II, 344.

[14] Sipos, *Enchiridion*, p. 305.

[15] Gregory of Nyssa. (395) *Adversus eos deferrunt Baptismum Oratio M. P. L.*, XLVI, 418; St. Ambrose, *Expositio Evangelii Lucae*, V, 76—*M. P. L.*, XV, 1634-35 (see Praesul in note at foot of page); St. Cyril of Jerusalem, *Procathecesis*, I, 4, 13—*M. P. G.*, XXXIII, 339.

[16] Saegmüller, Die Kirchenbücher in Kath. Deutschland, *T. Q. S.*, LXXXI (1899), 216.

2. *The Matrimonial Register Up to the Thirteenth Century*

Civil authorities in general demand that records of marriage be kept and "In several countries the civil law imposes the obligation of registering marriages, even in the baptismal register as a means of preventing bigamy or fraudulent unions. It is not surprising then that the Church should adopt similar measures since she is the guardian of the sacredness, unity and indissolubility of marriage." [17] The canonical matrimonial register is a most protective measure and "it is indispensable on account of the necessity of avoiding litigation. A full proof of the marriage is offered from this record, even though the witnesses have since died." [18]

The history of the matrimonial register depends in great part upon the evolution of the form of marriage and it was not until the Council of Trent that the substantial form of marriage was required. Before this no special form of solemnity was necessary for the valid celebration of the Christian marriage. From the canonical viewpoint consent alone sufficed and this was founded in the natural law. Accidental and secondary solemnities, however, were required in various places and at various times [19] an example of which shall be seen in the delineation of the register during this period.

The diptychs offer no preformations [20] but following the course of history attention is arrested by a ruling of the Emperor Justinian in his *Novellae*.[21] Herein his decree is declared to have been demanded by experience, and it has led him to rule that if a man and his concubine or a husband who had made a forbidden marriage with a girl of low estate [22] wishes to marry validly, without such instruments of proof as a dowry or prenuptial donation they should come to the church and before the defender or advocate and other witnesses profess their desire. After which a document was to be drawn

[17] Ayrinhac, *Marriage Legislation in the New Code of Canon Law*, p. 259.

[18] Baruffaldus, *Ad Rit. Roman. Comment.*, p. 450; Giraldi, *Addit. et. Animadv. ad Barbosam "De officio et Potestate Episcopi,"* part II, 22, n. 175.

[19] Wernz-Vidal, *Jus Matrimoniale*, 618.

[20] Sipos, *Enchiridion*, p. 305.

[21] *Novellae*, 74, 4, 1, 2.

[22] *Code of Theodosius IV*, 6, 3; Krueger-Mommsen, I (latter part), p. 176; Holmes, *Age of Justinian and Theodora*, I, p. 108.

up with signature, date, place, etc., so that in the eyes of the law this would prove the children legitimate. They could have such certificates if so desired, to which he adds:

> Sin vero etiam hoc illi non egerint, ille tamen talem reponat chartam venerabilis illius ecclesiae defensor in ejusdem sanctissimae ecclesiae archivis (ubi vasa venerabilia servantur) praedictas subscriptiones habentem, ut reconditum sit hominibus ex hoc munimen.

The *defensor ecclesiae* was usually a priest [23] and acted as a publim official.[24] Rittershuttius [25] in comment says this regulation of Justinian's was a remedy for legal illegitimacy. The commentator goes on to say that consent to marry was sufficient and such proving instruments as prenuptial donations were accidentals, affecting not at all the substance of the marriage. Practically, therefore, here is had no ecclesiastical register but an example of the concurrent action of Church and State for special cases in that period, which concurrence has been pointed out previously.

3. *The Book of the Dead Up to the Thirteenth Century*

The Code, having laid down the rules concerning death and burial, prescribes a practical means of keeping records of the entirety.[26] The identity of the deceased, the time of death, what Sacraments were administered and by whom, the time and the place of burial, all are to be recorded in a book designated as the Register of the Dead. This is to be preserved in the parish and cared for by those who are in charge.

The same situation prevails in regards to this register as has been seen in relation to the others. Again there is had a preformation but the relation of the diptychs of the dead to the present register is not at all striking. Probably the prime purpose of the former was not the same as motivates the prescription of the latter, however some secondary connection between the two is apparent.

[23] Ferraris, Advocatus Ecclesiae, *Prompt. Bibliotheca,* I, 143.

[24] Sherman, *Roman Law in the Modern World,* I, 130.

[25] C. Rittershuttius, *Methodica Expositio Novellae,* IV, 247, 248, ns. 11-15.

[26] Canon 1238.

Cabrol [27] speaking of this record declares it was reserved for those who died in the faith. Probably it gave no more detailed account than the names. The chief purpose was that the inscribed be remembered in the Mass [28] and on the anniversary of the death.[29] At times it was limited to the names of important persons,[30] a general commemoration of the rest being made.[31]

Saints Cyprian and Dionysius the Areopagite bear sufficient witness to this record. The former declares that for the violation of conciliar decrees the offender, though dead, should not have sacrifice offered for him [32] and in Epistle 37 he asks that the names of the dead be sent that they be inscribed and sacrifice offered for them." In the book attributed to Dionysius the Areopagite this register is shown in a somewhat wider perspective *"Sacrarum porro tabularum quae post pacem adhibetur recitatio, depraedicat eos qui sancte vixerunt, atque ad probae vitae perfectionem constanter pervenerunt . . ."* [34]

4. *Register of the "Status Animarum" Up to the Thirteenth Century*

The fifth book explicitly prescribed by the Code is more general in the nature than the rest. This register is one calculated to keep the clergy in close contact with those in their charge. It is not easy to give a more detailed account of this register here since it would be an infringement, more or less, upon the commentary. Suffice it to say that this book is the complement of the others and as the Council of Trent [35] so aptly puts it the idea motivating this mandate is *"melius agnoscere oves."*

[27] "Diptychon," *Dict. de Lit. et d'Arch. Chrit.*, IV, I, 1050.

[28] *Cath. Encycl.* V, 23 sq.

[29] Saegmüller, Die Kirchenbücher in Kath. Deutschland—*T. Q. S.*, LXXXI (1899), 216 ss.

[30] Smith & Cheetham, *Dictionary of Christian Antiquities*, p. 56 ss.

[31] Bona, *Rer. Liturg.*, II, XII, 1, p. 390 ss.; Selvagio, *Instit. Antiq. Christ.*, II, II, II, p. 77.

[32] Epistle LXVI—*M. P. L.*, IV, 398, 399 (see note of Stephen Baluzius at foot of page).

[33] Epistle XXXVII—*M. P. L.*, IV, 327-329.

[34] *De Eccles. Hier.*, III, IX—*M. P. L.*, III, 438.

[35] Sess. XXIII, *de ref.*, Canon 1.

Once again a search is made into the primitive Church to ascertain whether or not any such record was had at that time. In the diptychs of the living can be recognized in barest outline, the register known today. This quasi-register took its origin from the inscribing of the names of those offering for the Holy Sacrifice and as such was read at the Mass.[36] "In the early Christian ages it was customary to write on diptychs the names of those who were considered members of the Church—hence the terms diptychs of the living." [37]

A few instances may be cited here in corroboration of these diptychs as quasi-registers. "The use of these diptychs (including the *libri vivorum*) is attested to by the writings of St. Cyprian (third century) and by the history of St. John Chrysostom (fourth century)." [38] Cyril of Jerusalem (386) conveys the idea that it had become a proof of orthodoxy *"Vidis Scripturarum lectionem, canonicarum (seu in tabulis ecclesiasticis inscriptarum) personarum praesentiam."* [39] In the fifth century the diptychs of the living were still in use.[40] After this virtually no trace of them survives, though the *Catholic Encyclopedia* [41] maintains they existed until the twelfth century in the West and the fourteenth century in the East.

All that has preceded cannot be considered as extremely pertinent; the next period brings definite landmarks, however, and the present writer has thought its importance sufficient to warrant inclusion here, because of its performatory character.

Article III

Parish Registers in the Jus Novum

Prior to the enactments of the Council of Trent particular legislative bodies drew up measures to secure the maintenance of the

[36] Smith & Cheetham, *Dictionary of Christian Antiquities*, p. 561 sq; Bona, *Rer. Liturg.*, II, XII, I, 390 sq.

[37] "Diptych," *Cath. Encycl.*, V, 23.

[38] *Ut supra.*

[39] Procatechesis, I, 4—*M. P. G.*, XXXIII, 339.

[40] Mabillion, *Bened. Praefatio ad V saeculum*, n. 97, p. 416.

[41] V, p. 23.

parochial books, but the first general legislation is not found until that Ecumenical Council.

1. *The Glossators*

The *Corpus Juris Canonici* is the first body of legislation to engage attention. It is, however, only in an indirect way that matters of interest are to be found herein. The work itself yields no immediate sources in this connection and hence the inquiry must be directed to its commentaries of the thirteenth, fourteenth and fifteenth centuries.

Three of the so-called glossators [42] offer references to some proving instruments in the case of marriage. Bernard of Pavia whose *Summa* was made between 1191-1198, deplores in this work [43] clandestine marriages, though admittedly legal and binding, because the denial by one party sufficed to render the marriage, in the eyes of the law, nonexistent, since neither witnesses nor instrument of proof was had. A bare statement, most indefinite for the purpose here, is the sum total of his effort in this matter. All that can be shown is the fact that some probatory record (instrument) was maintained.

The *Summa* of Hostiensis (about 1251) [44] sheds a little more light on the subject. He declares in this place *"Pro hac autem benedictione nihil exigi debet obtentu etiam alicujus consuetudinis, nec pro charta,"* an indication that some ecclesiastical recording of the marriage was incumbent upon the priest assisting.

Finally, one of the latest glossators, Nicholas de Tudeschis, better known as Panormitanus (1453) [45] in considering the problem of the proof from instruments, gives a better insight into the matter. He avows that all such records are not of full proof and as Esmein [46] and Wernz [47] see it, he declares that the record of marriages pre-

[42] Wernz-Vidal, *De Matrimonio,* p. 663.

[43] *Summa Papiensis,* pp. 141, 142.

[44] *Summa Hostiensis,* tome IV, *de secund. nuptiis,* p. 375.

[45] *Summa,* p. 47 ss. (commentary on 13, X ad probat., II, 19).

[46] *Le Mariage in Droit Canonique,* I, 193-195.

[47] Wernz-Vidal, *De Matrimonio,* p. 663.

served at that time could not be held unqualifiedly as of full probative value. It was considered chiefly as a private writing necessitating the support of witnesses. Panormitanus [48] however holds otherwise in regard to the baptismal register. He observes that the record of baptism demands recognition as full proof because it is reserved in public and faithful custody (in the bishop's residence) and generally is *in nullius praejudicio,* which opinion Esmein [49] supports. The nonparochial character of the record is easily explained. For many centuries the solemn conferring of Baptism was exclusively an episcopal function and only certain churches enjoyed the right to maintain baptismal fonts.[50]

2. *Particular Councils Before the Council of Trent*

The IV Lateran Council (1215 A. D.) under the guidance of Innocent III was in all probability, the motivating cause behind the introductions of the first decrees concerning parochial books. In the twenty-first Canon, *Omnis Utriusque Sexus Fidelis,* of this Council were joined the prescriptions on Confession and annual Communion.[51] The contents of this Canon, were delineated with such clarity and forcefulness [52] that a very deep impression was made upon the mind of the times. In view of this, it is not surprising to see, somewhat later, the book of the *status animarum* come into use as a measure calculated to facilitate the enforcement of the decree concerning Confession and Communion.

Among the enactments of the Council of Beziers held in 1286 A. D.[53] is discovered what appears to be the first legislation on the registers, which regulations resulted from the activity initiated by the famous twenty-first Canon of the IV Lateran Council. Not only was consideration given to those who fulfilled the prescription

[48] *Summa,* IV, 47 (comment. on C. 13, X, de probat. II, 18).

[49] Esmein, *op. cit.,* I, 193-195.

[50] Selvagio, *Inst. Antiq. Christ.,* IV, II, II, 84; Catalanus, *Rit. Roman. Benedict XIV,* I, 32; II, 344; C. XVI, q. I, Canon 54, 55.

[51] C. Laternan, IV, Canon 21—*Mansi,* XXII, 1007; Denzinger-Baanwart, *Enchiridion,* n. 437.

[52] Villien, *A History of the Commandments of the Church,* p. 204.

[53] C. Benz, Canon XIII—*Harduin,* VII, 954, 952.

Omnis Utriusque Sexus Fidelis but also those who failed in so doing were recorded as excommunicates. In the early part of the next century at Salamanca (1335) [54] it was ordered that such records were to be exhibited to the Ordinary at the time of his visitation. Finally a Council sitting at Toledo (1339) [55] promulgated the same law in a general way.

During the first part of the following century the book of the *status animarum* continued to be the only book concerning which legislation is found. In the Synod of Kammin in Germany (1454) [56] a decree was issued for the preservation of a book of the excommunicated and interdicted. The latter half of the fifteenth century brought forth legislation of much importance in the history of these books. Two synods held at Constance (1463 A. D. and 1483 A. D.) published the same decree which reads thus:

> . . . Hujusmodi periculis (matrimonial impediments) cupientes quo ad nobis subjectos obviare, decernimus et hoc statuto perpetuo servari praecipimus, ut Ecclesiarum per civitatem et diocesim, nostros rectores, plebani, vici-plebani et singuli curati in baptizando pueros subditorum suorum, levantium et baptizati nomina in registro communi, quod in sua Ecclesia habeant, conscribant, et testes quamplures assumant; similiter . . . in confirmatione . . . , ut facilius impedimenta hujusmodi et minoribus laboribus et expensis valeant opportuno tempore comprobari.[57]

Here is a definite step forward, the books of the baptized and the confirmed are prescribed and a reason is offered for the institution of these registers, the matrimonial impediment of spiritual relationship. This is the initial appearance of the confirmation register and the word "common" is applied to the books probably denoting the kind of registers to be considered shortly, concerning which Saegmüller [58]

[54] C. Salaman., cap. 16, n. 41—*Harduin,* VII, 1974.

[55] C. Toletan., Canon 5—*Harduin,* VII, 1638.

[56] Synodus Camin.,—*Concil. German.,* V, 935.

[57] C. Constant., c. X—*Concil. German.,* V, 456 (for that of 1463); *Concil. German.,* V, 552 (for that of 1483).

[58] Die Kirchenbücher in Kath. Deutschland—*T. Q. S.,* LXXXI (1899), pp. 227, 240, 247.

speaks. Nearly fifty years later the same legislative precept can be recognized among those promulgated at Hildesheim (1539).[59]

The evolution now moves forward in a surprisingly rapid manner. At Augsburg (1548) a tremendous expansion of the idea is to be noted. Four books are the subjects of enactments here:

> Parochi seu presbyteri curati omnes, libros apud ecclesias suas habeant quattuor; primum, in quo baptizatorum: secundum, in quo statuto ab ecclesia tempore confitentium et communicantium: tertium, in quo eorum qui matrimonium in facie ecclesiae contraxerunt: et quartum, in quo mortuorum et ecclesiasticae sepulturae traditorum: nomina, cognomina cum annotatione diei et anni describantur. Haec enim diligentia cum ad multa utilis, tum vero ad hoc pracipue ut pastoribus ovium suarum ratio melius constat.[60]

Only the book of the confirmed has been neglected; the register of the deceased has entered clear upon the legislative field and the great influence of the Lateran decree can still be seen from the detailed attention given to the matter of the second book.[61]

[59] C. Hildesch., c. 11—*Concil. German.*, VI, 139.
[60] Synod. August., c. 8—*Mansi,* XXXII, 1302.
[61] C. August., cap. XIX—*Concil. Harduin,* IX, 2041.

CHAPTER III

PARISH REGISTERS FROM COUNCIL OF TRENT TO THE CODE

ARTICLE I

THE COUNCIL OF TRENT (1545-1563)

AMONG the outstanding performances of the Council of Trent was the radical modification wrought in matrimonial law. The great Reform Council made a solemnization (presence of the pastor) of marriage necessary for validity.[1] After this decision had been reached, the Fathers proceeded to adopt a measure, very simple, yet very important for the matter of proof.[2] Thus spoke the Council: *"Habeat parochus librum in quo conjugum et testium nomina diemque et locum contracti matrimonii describat quem apud se custodiat."* [3] A special and adequate proof of marriage was legislated into being, something which the ancient Canon Law had failed to provide, as the works of the glossators, already seen, have shown.[4]

In the following Canon [5] mindful of the spiritual impediment to matrimony arising from the sponsor relationship of baptism,[6] it was decreed:

> Parochus, antequam ad baptismum conferendum accedat, diligenter ab eis, ad quos spectabit, sciscitetur, quem vel quos elegerint, ut baptizatum de sacro fonte suscipiant, et eum vel eos tantum ad illud suscipiendum admittat et in libro eorum nomina describat, doceatque eos quam cognationem contraxerint . . .

[1] Esmein, *Le Mariage en Droit Canonique*, II, 154; Wernz-Vidal, *De Matrimonio*, 623 ss.

[2] Esmein, *op. cit.*, p. 188.

[3] C. Trident., Sess. XXIV, *de ref. matr.*, Canon 1—*Mansi*, XXXIII, 152, 153.

[4] Esmein, *Le Mariage en Droit Canonique*, II, 188.

[5] C. Trident., Sess. XXIV, *de ref. matr.*, Canon 2—*Mansi*, XXXIII, 153.

[6] Pallavicino, Sforza, *Istoria del Concilio di Trento*, IV, 594 (Rome, 1833).

With the promulgation of this decree the prescription of the baptismal register became a general law binding the Church.

Anent the marriage register there is an interesting ramification found here. It has been seen in the time of Justinian that the Church and State worked hand in hand in the matter of marriage records. In France, from 1539 A. D., a somewhat similar condition was found. The civil authorities recognized the ecclesiastical register, giving it a civil status, whence the name "mixed or common register" was derived. This state of affairs continued until the French Revolution came along and swept it into oblivion.[7] Esmein [8] considers this matter at some length, giving the civil statutes. In Germany, too, according to Saegmüller [9] this was not unknown and Van Espen [10] gives an explicit example of the civil regulation in connection with an annual report on the ecclesiastical records, not only of marriage but of baptisms and deaths as well.

Article II

Post-Tridentine Conciliar Legislation

The Post-Tridentine Period is the most important legislative era for registers, encompassing an extensive and detailed evolution through the medium of Councils, the Roman Ritual, decrees of the Roman Pontiffs and the Sacred Congregations. The clearer conceptions are examples of the progressive spirit of legislation during this period of outstanding development before the Code.

1. *Milanese Councils of St. Charles Borromeo*

To a series of six councils held at Milan (1565-1582) under the aegis of St. Charles Borromeo, that group of books, known today as parish registers, owe their origin, as a unit. Besides putting into effect the general laws of the Council of Trent, including those on the

[7] Wernz-Vidal, *De Matrimonio*, p. 664.

[8] *Le Mariage en Droit Canonique*, II, 188 sq.; 201 sq.

[9] Die Kirchenbücher in Kath. Deutschland—*T. Q. S.*, LXXXI (1899), pp. 227, 240, 247.

[10] *Jus Eccl. Univers.*, Part II, sect. I, t. XII, cap. VI, n. XXI.

baptismal and matrimonial registers [11] which was the chief purpose of said Councils, they encompassed in their legislative ambitus the three remaining books, those of the confirmed, dead and the *status animarum.* With regards to the book of the baptized some practical rules were laid down especially for the inscription of an illegitimate child. The First Council added the command to forward an annual report of baptisms to the Ordinary, who was held to preserve such records.[12] In the very next title the bishops were called upon to use all possible diligence that the pastors maintain a book of the confirmed, following as far as possible the regulations for the register of the baptized.

The IV Provincial Council incorporates under the title *Quae pertinent ad Sacramentum Poenitentiae* [13] the regulations for the book of the *status animarum* because it dealt with the inscription of those approaching the tribunal of Penance during the Paschal Season. Finally in the IV Council in the title *Quae pertinent ad Extreman Unctionem et Reliqua erga morientes Officia* [14] it was made incumbent upon the pastors to report monthly to the Rural Dean or the Regional Prefect those who have died during that time and all things concerning their care during sickness and after the death. As a fitting conclusion of these matters, it was ruled in the title *De* Visitatione [15] that these records were to be preserved by the pastor in an archive or secure place in the sacristy, and were to be at hand when the bishop came on visitation.[16]

2. *Legislation of Other Particular Councils*

During the period of the Milanese Councils other legislative bodies showed activity in the same matters. The book of *status ani-*

[11] *Acta Ecclesiae Mediolanensis* (A. E. M.), Tome I, Part I, Actorum Concilii Provincialis IV, part III, De Concilio Provinciali, pp. 8, 109; *op. cit.,* pp. 35, 84.

[12] (I Council), *A. E. M.,* Tome I, part I, p. 8.

[13] (IV Council), *A. E. M.,* Tome I, part II, p. 114 (col. 1).

[14] (IV Council), *A. E. M.,* Tome I, part II, p. 114 (col. 2).

[15] (IV Council), *A. E. M.,* Tome I, part III, p. 142 (col. 1).

[16] (IV Council), *A. E. M.,* Tome I, part III, p. 143 (col. 1).

marum was much in evidence.[17] The decrees of the Synod of Augsburg (1548) seem to have influenced mightily the Council sitting at Rouen (1581) [18] since the same four books were demanded in practically the same words. At Bordeaux (1583) [19] two years later again four parish registers were required; the neglected book in each of the above conciliar rulings being that of the *status animarum*. The same was true of Avignon.[20]

The matter of the preservation of the parochial books was the chief consideration of the Council of Cambrai (1586).[21] This legislative body demanded that an archive be used for preservation of such records, if the church was a collegiate one; if a parish church then the sacristan was to care for the books. The privilege of inspection was had only by the pastor and parties to whom it would be of special interest. The above regulations applied chiefly to the baptismal and matrimonial records. The only other book prescribed was that in which the shriven and communicants were entered. The Council added to this a rule that the names of the nonconfessing and noncommunicating should be sent to the bishop. At Toulouse (1589) [22] ending the same decade, the Council sitting there was particularly interested in the record of the *status animarum*.

A convocation gathered at Salerno (1599) [23] issued very detailed instructions on the parochial books. The five registers were prescribed. To the mandate concerning the baptismal register, was added, beyond the usual regulations, a few words of instruction concerning the recording of a spurious child. It was directed that the mother's name, at least, should be entered. The register of the *status animarum* was to contain, not only the record of the fulfillment of the obligation of Confession and Communion but the condition of the whole parish was to be inscribed. Each year the bishop

[17] C. Mechlin., *Harduin,* X, 1181 (1570)—*Mansi,* XXXVI, A, cols. 201-202, const. 26.

[18] C. Roth., *Harduin,* X, 1257.

[19] C. Burgdal., *Mansi,* XXXIV, A, 768.

[20] C. Avenion. (1594)—*Mansi,* XXXIV, B, 1354.

[21] C. Cameracen.—*Concil. German.,* VII, 1004, 1005, 1009.

[22] C. Tolosana.—*Harduin,* X, 1800.

[23] C. Salernit., *De Officio Parochi,* cap. X—*Mansi,* XXXV, B, 1008.

was to be made acquainted with the contents of the various registers, so that he might preserve the records in the diocesan archives. The final regulation admonishes the pastors to have care that no one secure any information from a register without the bishop's permission, unless it is a certificate of birth or age that is sought.

At Narbonne (1609) [24] the first conciliar legislation of the seventeenth century is found. This Council directed the maintenance of records of baptism, marriage, death, and if the Sacrament of Confirmation was conferred in the parish (not yet a very widespread practise) [25] the names of the confirmed were to be entered. All the entries were to be made in one book; however, each kind of register was to have a separate portion alloted to it. The *status animarum* was given a special book in which the names of the shriven were to be inserted.[26] In the following year several German Councils [27] prescribed various combinations of the registers but no one demanded the five to be kept.

Article III

The Parish Register from the Introduction of the Roman Ritual

A tremendous influence was exerted upon parish registers by the introduction of the Roman Ritual of Paul V in the year 1614. Through it a new status was acquired by those books which had not been incorporated in the body of legislation brought into being by the Council of Trent, namely, the registers of the confirmed, deceased and of the *status animarum*.

In the Bull *Apostolicae Sedis* of Paul V which accompanied his Ritual, the Supreme Pontiff declared that this book was to be used everywhere, by all and its prescriptions were to be fully observed.[28] Then in the very first title of the Ritual, *De Iis quae in Sacramen-*

[24] C. Narbonen.—*Mansi*, XXXIV, B, 1513.

[25] Catalanus, *Comment. ad Rit. Roman. Benedict XIV*, I, II, p. 344.

[26] C. Narbon., *Harduin*, XI, 17.

[27] C. Salizburg.—*Concil. German.*, VII, 1072; C. Warmen.—*Concil. German.*, IX, 106, 109, 135; C. August.—*Concil. German.*, IX, 70.

[28] *Bullarium Romanorum Pontificium*, XII, 266 (no. 251).

torum Administratione Generaliter Servanda sunt [29] it is stated that anyone held to administer the Sacraments ought to have the books pertinent to the duties, especially those in which the various parochial functions are to be inscribed for future reference. This certainly applies to the five parochial books [30] treated in the final title.[31]

The Roman Ritual produced a great effect toward the widespread establishment of the five books. This is seen in the legislation of councils, where enactments on such matters generally were introduced by the phrase *"secundum Rituale Romanum."* [32]

The definite place thus acquired by the registers was naturally productive of a more extensive and intensive consideration of the various books than had hitherto been given. Accordingly, the different aspects of the books can now be properly viewed. No longer does the legislation consider the registers merely *in globo,* from now on they receive more intensive and extensive individual consideration. From this time down to the Code of Canon Law, the various books have a more definitely separate entity and hence it is advantageous at this point to follow each book separately through the remainder of the pre-Code period, viewing each one in the light of any legislative changes wrought in its composition.

Article IV

Development of Particular Registers Down to the Code

1. *The Baptismal Register*

The first of the five books enumerated and given a formula in the last title of the Roman Ritual of Paul V [33] was that of the baptized,

[29] *Rit. Roman. Pauli V Pont. Max. Jussu Editum,* p. 4.

[30] Baruffaldus, *Commentarium ad Rit. Roman.* I, 33.

[31] *"Formulae Scribendae in libris habendis apud Parochos," Rit. Roman. Pauli V,* pp. 377, 383.

[32] C. Beneventana (1693), *Collect. Lacen.,* I, 72; C. Avenionensis (1725), *Collect. Lacen.,* I, 526, 583; C. Neapolit. (1699), *Collect. Lacen.,* I, 180; C. Colonien. (1745), *Concil. German.,* X, 529, 530, 550; C. Baltimore (1829) *Councils of Baltimore,* III, p. 30; C. Neogranatencis (1868), *Collect. Lacen.,* VI, 481.

[33] *Rit. Roman. Pauli V,* pp. 377-383.

which was to be maintained wherever a baptismal font was had. The dominant idea of the inscription prescribed therein seems to have been the recording of all the necessary information, yet noted in such a way as to preclude the accruement of any ill-fame to the parents of the one baptized.[34] Proper directions are given for the inscribing when a foundling is the subject of baptism. Conditional baptism, baptism *in periculo mortis* with the consequences incident to recovery, and the administration of this Sacrament by one other than the proper pastor are duly considered in the light of the registration. These constitute the Roman Ritual's contribution to the formation of the baptismal register as known today.

A rapid survey of the period from this time down to the Code, will be sufficient to indicate any changes which took place in the register under consideration. The revised Ritual of Benedict XIV in no way affected the record being considered here.[35] An encyclical epistle of the same Pontiff,[36] however, ruled that the children of marriages of conscience upon baptism were to be inscribed in a special and secret book kept in the archives of the chancery. Particular councils, on the other hand, manifested no progressive spirit with regards to new legislation, as witness the Councils of Baltimore [37] and those of Prague and Toulouse.[38] In a decree emanating from the Sacred Congregation of the Propaganda [39] a special book was brought into being for the inscription of the necessary information when certain grave difficulties made it incumbent upon a pastor to baptize a child belonging to another rite. In this book the fact of its belonging to a different rite was to be noted and the proper pastor was to be informed that Baptism had been administered.

The next legislation to be met with is of great importance. In

[34] *Op. cit.*, p. 377.

[35] *Cath. Encycl.*, "Roman Ritual," XIII, pp. 88-90.

[36] Benedict XIV, Encycl. Epist., *Satis Vobis*, November 14, 1741, n. 10—*Fontes*, n. 319.

[37] *Councils of Baltimore*, III, p. 30: The I Baltimore Council alone gave an extensive consideration to the registers; II and III virtually followed the prescriptions of the earliest Council held there.

[38] *C. Pragen.* (1860)—*Collect., Lacen.*, V, 563; *C. Tolsan.* (1850), *Collect., Lacen.*, IV, 1053.

[39] S. C. de P. F., October 6, 1863—*Collect. S. C. de Prop. Fide*, n. 1243.

this group, the final pre-Code legislation, may be recognized the reason for calling the baptismal register the "principal book" [40] today. In the famous decree *Ne Temere* on marriage [41] it was declared that an annotation of marriage was to be made in the baptismal register and if one party to the marriage had been baptized elsewhere, notice of the marriage should be sent to such parish that it might be there registered in the record of baptism. In 1910 and 1911 the Sacred Congregation of the Sacraments [42] followed up this matter with an interpretation and an instruction. The instruction of 1911 admonished Ordinaries to see that this prescription was carried out and in the event of the noncompliance of pastors, they were to impose canonical penalties.

The introduction of such legislation leads to an inquiry as to whether or not, prior to the Code, an analogous duty, with regards to reception of Sacred Orders, solemn religious profession and Confirmation was imposed upon pastors. The only indication of any regulation in the matter of Holy Orders is found in a constitution of Innocent XII (1694) [43] wherein it was prescribed that a record of the ordination be transmitted to the bishop of the place of origin, etc., of the newly-ordained. Nothing further was added, no specific determination which would give it any close similarity to the measure found in the Code of Canon Law.[44] A pre-Code origin of the registration of solemn profession is, by far, still less evident. The nearest approach to such a legislative act is to be found in the Decree of Gratian [45] where it is simply stated that the record of profession should not be allowed to disappear. No mention is made concerning an annotation of the same in the register of the baptized. Finally, no notation of Confirmation is discoverable.

[40] Vermeersch-Creusen, *Epitome*, I, 325.

[41] S. C. C., decree *Ne Temere*, August 2, 1907, art. X, 2 and 3—*A. S. S.*, XL (1907), 529.

[42] S. C. de Sacr., *Romana et aliarum*, March 12, 1910, n. 9—*A. A. S.*, II (1910), 194-195; S. C. de Sacr., March 6, 1911, n. 4—*A. A. S.*, III (1911), 102.

[43] Const., *Speculatores*, November 4, 1694, 3 sq.—*Fontes*, n. 258.

[44] Canon 1011.

[45] C. 35, C. XXVII, q. 1.

2. *The Register of the Confirmed*

To the prescription of the Roman Ritual of Paul V (1614)[46] must be attributed the extensive growth of this record. The final title of this work[47] indicates the notations to be made in the register of the confirmed. The males and females are to be on separate pages and the names of the sponsors are to be entered. Finally, not all churches were required to maintain such a record, only those wherein the Sacrament of Confirmation was administered.[48] Aside from this, the register of the confirmed has come down to the Code unaffected by the ecclesiastical legislation of nearly three hundred years.

3. *The Matrimonial Register*

In directing what information is to be inscribed in this book, the Roman Ritual of Paul V[49] in addition to the names of the contracting parties and the witnesses together with the subscription of the priest, demands that the pastor should take cognizance, in writing, of one or the other party's residence in a different parish or diocese. Especially when it is a question of the publishing of the banns, their deferring or omission. Also he should have a care that any dispensations issued for the contracting of marriage be suitably noted in the register.

During the pontificate of Benedict XIV a distinction was made concerning the recording of marriages. The Roman Pontiff[50] after stating what the Council of Trent[51] required in the way of matrimonial registers, took up the matter of marriages of conscience. The inscription of these, he declared, was to be made in a special book and to be preserved in the chancery archives.

[46] *Rit. Roman. Pauli V,* p. 377, sq.

[47] *Ibid.*

[48] *Op. cit.,* p. 377; Giraldi, *Animad et addiment. ad Barbosam "De officio et Potestate Parochi,"* I, cap. 7, p. 63.

[49] Title, *Forma Scribendi Conjugatos,* 379.

[50] Benedict XIV, encycl. epist., *Satis Vobis,* November 14, 1741, No. 10, ss.—*Fontes,* 319.

[51] Sess. XXIV, *de ref. matr.,* Canon 1.

In 1785 the Sacred Congregation of the Propaganda [52] issued a decree to solve the difficulties of inscription arising from a marriage which necessity or great need of the contracting parties had compelled entrance into while the priest was absent, as is the case in missionary countries. It was directed that the parties to the marriage must make known the fact to the priest as soon as possible and he, in turn, was secretly (because of civil regulations) to enter the marriage, the names of the witnesses and the date in the register.

The next piece of legislation on this book emanated from the same Congregation [53] in the year 1791 and dealt with the matter of the matrimonial dispensations. In this decree again the Tridentine law on the registration was reviewed to which the Congregation added that the pastor must enter in the same book a record of any dispensation secured from the impediments to matrimony.

Finally, the legislation before the Code on the matrimonial register, is concluded with a rather important addition to the law. The decree *Ne Temere* and an interpretation and instruction on the same [55] by the Sacred Congregation of the Sacraments comprise this addition. Since they have been reviewed in connection with the baptismal register, no more detailed notice need be given them here. Suffice it to say in conclusion that this was an important step in the history of the parish registers and one calculated to bring the two outstanding parochial books in closer relation to each other. In this connection it might not be amiss to recall that the Fathers of the Council of Trent saw in the baptismal record a practical aid to the celebration of valid marriages, and in view of this demanded its maintenance.[56] Here again in the twentieth century, matrimony makes felt its influence upon the baptismal register.

[52] S. C. de P. F., *Instructio Praefecto Missionum Insulae Curacao—Collect. S. C. de P. F.*, n. 571.

[53] S. C. de P. F., *Instructio,* Ad Epis. Hibern., June 25, 1791—*Collectanea S. C. de P. F.*, n. 605.

[54] S. C. C., August 2, 1907, art. IX, 1, 2, 3—*A. S. S.*, XL (1907), 529.

[55] S. C. de Sacr., "*Romana et Aliarum,*" March 12, 1910—*A. A. S.*, II (1910), 194, 195; S. C. de Sacr., "*Romana et Aliarum,*" March 6, 1911—*A. A. S.*, III (1911), 102.

[56] Pallavicino, *Istoria Del Concilio di Trento,* IV, 594.

4. *The Book of the Dead*

"Liber Defunctorum habeatur etiam in omnibus Ecclesiis in quibus defuncti sepeliuntur," says the Roman Ritual of Paul V.[57] This register, according to the final title of the same work [58] is to contain not only the name of the deceased, but also that of the family, together with an enumeration of the Sacraments received and by whom they were conferred. It also directed that the date of death as well as the place of burial were to be inscribed, even though the burial was not in the parish church. The reason offered for such a record being that the pastor might ever be able to give proper testimony to anyone seeking knowledge of a death.[59]

Aside from some provincial conciliar legislation [60] which depended greatly for its details upon the Ritual, ecclesiastical legislation with the death records as its direct and sole object is virtually indiscoverable. Its inclusion in the general group makes its history similar to that of the register of the confirmed and the prescriptions of the Roman Rituals of Paul V and Benedict XIV must be recognized as the vehicles that carried it down to the Code of Canon Law.

5. *The Register of the "Status Animarum"*

The great solicitude of the Council of Trent [61] for the proper care of souls found an admirable complement in the Roman Ritual of Paul V.[62] In prescribing the maintenance of such a book a detailed account was given of those things the pastor should inscribe in this record.[63] Each family in the parish was to be alloted a given amount

[57] P. 377.

[58] P. 383.

[59] Giraldi, *Animad. et addiment. ad Barbosam "De officio et Potestate Parochi,"* I, 63, n. 11.

[60] C. Gandav. (1650)—*Concil. German.*, IX, 722; C. Ruraemundensis (1652)—*Concil. German.*, IX, 781; C. Colonien. (1649)—*Concil. German.*, IX, 686; C. Eichstalt. (1700)—*Concil. German.*, X, 268; C. Colonien. (1745)—*Concil. German.*, X, 529; C. Burdigal (1850)—*Collect. Lacen.*, IV, 574.

[61] SS. XXIII, *de ref.*, Canon 1.

[62] Giraldi, *Animad. et Addiment. ad Barbosam "De officio et Potestate Parochi,"* 1, VII, 61, n. 1.

[63] *Rit. Roman. Pauli V*, p. 382.

of space wherein the full name, age and family relation of the individual members were to be inscribed. Also, the removal of a given family or person was to be indicated in the record. Special signs were employed to indicate the spiritual standing of the persons enrolled, especially with regard to Communion, First and Paschal, and Confirmation.

During this period among other things is noted a definite change in the register under consideration. Until now, the *status animarum* record had dealt chiefly with the matter of the inscription of those who confessed annually. The Roman Ritual gives no place for the continuance of such a practice; instead one of the chief concerns of the book is to have gathered within its covers information pertaining to the fulfillment of the precept on Paschal Communion.[64] Perhaps the following will suffice to explain in some wise this change. A long struggle had ensued between the secular and the regular clergy, whose privileges had greatly empowered them, in regard to the matter of the right to hear the annual confession of the parishioners. For a long time the pastors sought to maintain their sole right to this office, but it was a losing fight and at length they were forced to yield.[65] Hence the era of the registrations of the confessing closed. The rights of the pastors and the parish church, on the other hand, have been better maintained with regard to the Paschal Communion.[66] Thus, it is but natural to expect the changing over to this more workable method of insuring the compliance with the precept.

No outstanding modifications or additions to the prescriptions of the Ritual are to be found in succeeding legislation down to the Code of Canon Law. Conciliar legislation continues to lay down laws concerning the maintenance of the books, in general, with the Roman Ritual as the background and supporting principle. An instruction of the Sacred Congregation of the Propaganda Fide in 1869 [67] is indicative of the mind of the Church even after the pas-

[64] P. 382.

[65] Villien, *History of the Commandments of the Church*, pp. 176-182.

[66] Villien, *op cit.*, p. 222.

[67] S. C. de P. F., *Instr. Ad Vic. Apost. Indiar. Orient.*, September 8, 1869, n. 21—*Collect. S. C. de P. F.*, n. 1345.

sage of a century and a half. It declares, after prescribing the four other books in accordance with the Roman Ritual "*nec non diligenter curari recensionem status animarum et adimplementi praecepti paschalis.*"

PART III

CANONICAL EXPOSITION

CHAPTER IV

THE BAPTISMAL REGISTER

THE register of the baptized is the principal record among the group known as the parochial books.[1] Its extensive content, notably the various annotations required by the Code of Canon Law [2] renders it such. For purposes of commentary, the time of inscription of the various entries divides the content into two parts. The first concerns itself with the recordng of the fact of baptism, while the second includes the various canonically required additions to the same record, following, for instance, the reception of other Sacraments.

There is little need to apply to this book the measure of purpose. Registration of baptism establishes documentary proof of membership in the society of the Church, thereby positing in the external forum the fundamental requisite for subsequent ecclesiastical actions.

The regulations demanding the annotations indicate that the legislator foresaw with a practical eye that future activities, sacramental or no, of many members would have place elsewhere than in the church of baptism. Such being the case, a facile and accurate investigation of an individual's status would be very difficult. To prevent the arising of such conditions, the baptismal register, by means of the required additions, has become, as it were, a briefer and alternate source of inquiry concerning the status of a member of the Church, particularly when it is a question of the free state required for entrance to matrimony.[3] Augustine [4] declares that this the most complicated of the parochial books has the extra columns or rubrics to make these additional insertions because Holy Orders and solemn religious profession are diriment impediments to matrimony. The same is true of previous undissolved marriage.[5] The re-

[1] Vermeersch-Creusen, *Epitome,* I, n. 510.

[2] Canons 470, § 2, 777, 798, 1011, 576, 1103, 1988.

[3] Cocchi, *Commentarium,* III, n. 350.

[4] *A Commentary on the New Code of Canon Law,* II, 557.

[5] Canons 1069, § 1; 1072, 1073.

quiring of the inscription concerning Confirmation in the register of baptism is not motivated by any precautionary idea with regard to marriage but is founded upon the impossibility of this Sacrament's repetition [6] and other juridical consequences.[7]

ARTICLE I

INITIAL INSCRIPTION OF THE BAPTISMAL REGISTER

Canon 777, § 1. Parochi debent nomina baptizatorum, mentione facta de ministro, parentibus ac patrinis, de loco ac die collati baptismi, in baptismali libro sedulo et sine ulla mora referre.

§ 2. Ubi vero de illegitimis filiis agatur, matris nomen est inserendum, si publice ejus maternitas constet, vel ipsa sponte sua scripto vel coram duobus testibus id petat; item nomen patris, dummodo ipse sponte sua a parocho vel scripto vel coram duobus testibus id requirat, vel ex publico authentico documento sit notus; in ceteris casibus inscribatur natus tamquam filius patris ignoti vel ignotorum parentum.

Canon 778. Si baptismus nec a proprio parocho nec eo praesente administratus fuerit, minister de ipso collato quamprimum proprium ratione domicilii parochum baptizati ceteriorem reddat.

The above designated Canons embody the norms of procedure for the pastor in his capacity of an ecclesiastical notary recording officially and legally the fact of baptism.[8]

Inscription of the place and the date of baptism, minor matters from the viewpoint of extensiveness of commentary, are required for the authenticity of the document.[9] The date of birth, however, it must be remembered is not essential since neither the Code of Canon

[6] Canon 732, § 1.

[7] Blat. *Commentarium,* III, n. 95.

[8] Vermeersch-Creusen, *Epitome,* III, n. 77; Blat, *Commentarium,* III, n. 655.

[9] Blat, *Commentarium,* III, n. 68.

Law [10] nor civil law [11] accepts the baptismal record as conclusive proof of birth. The date of baptism, on the other hand, must always be recorded. Usually there will be no specific need to inscribe the place of baptism since ordinarily the register itself will supply that information. In the event that a church or place other than the proper church has been the scene of the administration then the parochial record of the parish must be inscribed to that effect. If another parochial church, with permission or for a just cause, is the place of baptism the record is to be inscribed there.

Canon 777, § 1, mentions two other comparatively unimportant details, in the light of canonical comment, namely, the manner and the time of entry. The former is circumscribed by the word *sedulo,* the import of which is that the entry should include all the canonically prescribed information set forth clearly and legibly.[12] The time of inscription is subject to qualification. The determination made by law is not numerical, and wisely so, since circumstances may influence the inscription's time-limit. Barring the concurrence of preventing circumstances, the inscription should follow immediately upon the administration of the Sacrament.[13] When some delay is imperative Augustine would not have a day intervene save in the case of a missionary who is traveling without the proper book in his immediate possession.[14] This, however, is somewhat too stringent, it appears, and a wider interpretation may be admitted in view of the fact that the law purposes to prevent an undue delay which would result in the neglect of the inscription or the loss of the required information with a consequent prejudice to the one baptized.

1. *The Minister*

Inclusion of the name of the minister is required because he is the special and the principal witness concerning those things necessary for the validity of the Sacrament.[15] When a lay person has admin-

[10] Canon 1816, *directe et principaliter . . . affirmantur.*

[11] Zollmann, *American Church Law,* No. 644, p. 592.

[12] Augustine, *Commentary,* IV, 95; Blat, *Commentarium,* III, n. 68.

[13] Blat, *ibid.*

[14] Augustine, *ibid.*

[15] Blat, *Commentarium,* III, n. 68.

istered the Sacrament an added reason is had since such a performance has given rise to the matrimonial impediment of spiritual relationship.[16] Ordinarily the one upon whom the onus of inscription falls will also be the minister, since to the proper pastor of the subject is reserved the right to confer solemnly the Sacrament of Baptism.[17] Nevertheless a number of circumstances may be verified in actual practise wherein the proper pastor and the minister are distinct persons. In such cases the name of the minister is to be inscribed [18] and not that of the pastor of the church. Even the name of the priest who assisted at the supplying of the ceremonies consequent to a private baptism is to be recorded.[19] In practise, said circumstances may involve the administration by a pastor other than the one of the place; again, performance of the baptism by a delegated priest, or by a lay person in case of necessity. How, then, are the canonical regulations concerning the inscription to be carried out in these situations?

If the proper pastor, by reason of domicile or quasi-domicile [20] does not confer the Sacrament or is not present, at least, at the time, it is incumbent upon the minister [21] to bring full knowledge of his administration to the proper pastor, as soon as possible, either personally or by mail.[22] Hence, such a one is required to obtain the same information as the pastor ordinarily secures prior to the registration. Fanfani [23] declares, however, in such a case it is not necessary to notify directly the proper pastor but it suffices for the minister to render the pastor of the place wherein the baptism was performed cognizant of its administration. He, in turn, can forward the secured information to the proper pastor of the subject.

The time within which this transmission is to be made depends

[16] Canons 1079, 768; Payen, *De Matrimonio*, n. 1564, 5.

[17] Canon 462, 1°.

[18] Canon 777, § 1; *Rit. Roman*, XII, II, p. 508.

[19] *Rit. Roman, ibid.*

[20] Canons 92, 94. For *vagi* the pastor of their present location is the proper pastor. Canon 94, § 2; Cappello, *De Sacramentis*, I, n. 188, 4.

[21] Priest or deacon in solemn or private conferring; layman in private administration. Blat, *Commentarium*, III, n. 69.

[22] Canon 778; Capello, *De Sacramentis*, I, n. 188, 4.

[23] *De Jure Parochorum*, n. 244, D.

upon the interpretation of *quam primum* had in Canon 778. Gasparri,[24] commenting upon the registration of marriages which validly can be applied here also, declares three or four days is the widest extension this term may have. Other authors avoid a numerical definition, confining themselves to the exclusion of voluntary procrastination.[25] Blat, while upholding the gravity of the obligation, is of the opinion that a few days delay ordinarily will be a light matter. He adds, however, at times it may be grave if the knowledge or certitude of a valid baptism is endangered by an even briefer delay.[26] The transference of such notifications can be made directly to the canonically appointed pastor or, especially when there is question of another diocese, through the diocesan curia.[27] This notification takes the form of an official document with pastoral signature and parochial seal, not a mere private letter. When one has been delegated to baptize the pastor should secure the necessary information from the minister and make the proper entries in the register. If he allows another to attend to the recording the pastor himself confirms the inscription with his signature.[28]

2. *The Name of the Baptized*

Occupying the first place in order in the baptismal register is the name of the person. The necessity of such an entry is perfectly obvious and no reasons need be adduced for its inclusion. Canon 761 directs the pastor to see that a Christian name is given the child. This, none the less, is not a strict obligation [29] because the parents or guardians have the right to bestow the name. In the event that they cannot be persuaded to impose a Christian name the minister adds a saint's name, inscribing both names in the register of the baptized.[30] In the case of a foundling, the name will be supplied usually by the organization handling the case. Incidentally this same source

[24] *De Matrimonio,* II, p. 171.
[25] Blat, *Commentarium,* III, n. 506; Augustine, *Commentary,* V, p. 312.
[26] *Commentarium,* III, n. 69.
[27] Augustine, *Commentary,* V, 313.
[28] Vermeersch-Creusen, *Epitome,* II, n. 55.
[29] Cappello, *De Sacramentis,* I, n. 179.
[30] Canon 761.

is to be utilized for the rest of the information required for inscription by Canon 777, § 1. The date of finding, the place, by whom found and the probable age [31] will suffice for inscription.

If it should happen that the child baptized, for any reason at all, belongs to another rite, a separate book, if necessary, should be had for such inscriptions [32] and the proper pastor of the same should be informed concerning the fact of baptism.[33] However, scarcely ever will the number of such cases demand a separate book, hence the usual book is used noting the fact of diverse rite therein.

3. *The Godparents*

The Code of Canon Law [34] demands that there be a witness or witnesses to the solemn conferring of Baptism and, though less emphatically, desires the same for private baptism. These persons, commonly called godparents, in their capacity of witnesses have a definite standing in the law in regard to the child baptized,[35] and one might say that it is chiefly because of the matrimonial impediment of spiritual relationship [36] which arises from this relation that the inscription of their names is required.[37]

Viewing the matter from this point cases can be visualized where it would not be strictly necessary to enter the names of such sponsors. Canon 763, § 2, declares that if the same godparents were used in a previous and then in a conditional baptism then the impediment arises. Therefore the employment of different persons in each ceremony leaves the same free from contracting the impediment with the baptized. Again, he who so acts merely for the supplying of the

[31] *Rit. Roman.*, XII, II, 507.

[32] Augustine, *Commentary*, IV, 95.

[33] S. C. P. F., October 6, 1863—*Collectanea S. C. de Prop. Fide*, n. 1243.

[34] Canons 762, § 1; 764; 762, § 2.

[35] Canons 768, 769.

[36] Canon 1079.

[37] C. Trident., sess. XXIV. *de ref. matr.*, c. 2—*Mansi* XXXIII, 153; Pallavicino, *Istoria del concilio di Trento*, IV, 594; C. Constant., c. X—*Concil. German.*, V, 456, 552; Blat, *Commentarium*, III, n. 68.

In private baptism the opinion is at least certain that the same impediment arises. Payen, *De Matrimonio*, I, n. 1568. There is some question concerning this point, however Canon 762, § 2, seems to stand strongly against a pre-Code opinion to the contrary, which depended mostly upon extrinsic probability.

ceremonies is not included in the category of the impeded.[38] Hence, under such conditions, from the viewpoint of the matrimonial impediment, there is no strict obligation to record such persons as sponsors. It would be better to enter the names of the godparents in such a case, indicating however that the impediment is not present.

4. *The Parents*

The greatest difficulty to be encountered in baptismal registration is found in the matter of parental inscription. The ordinary case demands no particular attention though it is well to remember that the recording of the place of family residence which the Code does not mention is of importance.[39] Also the obtaining of this important information along with the other details, prior to performing the ceremony will, at times, in actual practise save the minister from infringing upon the canonical rights of other pastors with regard to the baptism of subjects.

There are two possible circumstances surrounding a baptism, however, which must have special consideration when it is a question of parental inscription. The first may be verified in cases of illegitimacy and the second when the progeny are the issue of marriages of conscience.[40] The mode of procedure in the former case shall be discussed first, then the question of how this extraordinary marriage affects the parental inscription shall be considered.

It has long been the purpose of ecclesiastical legislation when dealing with the inscription of parents' names to provide that no ill-fame accrue to the parents of an illegitimate child. The caution urged in this regard in conciliar legislation [41] and in the Roman Ritual from its inception [42] has found a full expression in the Code [43] which de-

[38] Canon 762, § 2.

[39] *Rit. Roman.*, XII, II, p. 507; Fanfani, *De Jure Parochorum*, p. 415 (Formula XIII).

[40] Canons 1104-1107.

[41] Acts of the IV Provincial Council of Milan, III, *De Concilio Provinciali*, pp. 8, 109—A. E. M., I, I; C. Salernit., *De Officio Parochi*, c. X—*Mansi*, XXXV, B, 1008.

[42] *Rit. Roman., Pauli V*, p. 377.

[43] Canon 777, § 2.

clares as a general rule that illegitimate children are to be inscribed as the offspring of unknown parents. The phrase *parentum ignotorum* reducing as far as possible the arising of any scandalous knowledge and ill-fame from the fact that a child is adulterine, sacrilegious or otherwise spurious.[44]

Canon Law considers the problem of inscription here from two points. It considers the legal identification of the mother of the child, then that of the father. In fine, the verification of various circumstances in the case of each parent governs the norm of procedure.

Canon 777, § 2, declares that the mother's name must remain unknown to the record unless the knowledge of her motherhood is public or, when her maternity is not publicly known, she is desirous of being registered as the mother, which intention is brought to the pastor's notice, either in writing or before two witnesses. The latter part of this regulation is introduced to protect the pastor from libel action later. It is only through the medium of these two rules that the pastor is to be guided in deciding upon the legality of inscribing the mother's name.

A decision as to whether or no the maternity of the child is publicly known will probably be necessary in the greater number of cases. The other and easier classification is of rarer occurrence. The pastor, therefore, must be prepared to compare the circumstances present in a given case with the canonically constituting elements of a public fact.[45] The law [46] merely outlines in a general manner what these elements are. Has the knowledge already been divulged or from a prudent judgment does it appear that the conditions point to future publishment? If either of these are verified, actual or virtual divulgation, the maternity is public and the record to be made.

From this the question naturally arises concerning the number of

[44] Fanfani, *De Jure Parochorum*, n. 244, B, a; Com. ad C. C. Auth. Interp., July 14, 1922—*A. A. S.*, XIV (1922), 528.

[45] Since elsewhere in the Code no deciding regulation can be found concerning a public fact, the force of Canon 20 must be invoked whereby the principles of Canon 2197, which is concerned with delicts, can be applied here to a question of fact.

[46] Canon 2197, 1°.

people who must be acquainted with the fact before one can declare it public. This appears to be a purely relative matter.[47] The size of the place, the number and the quality of those having the knowledge must determine the decision. Vermeersch-Creusen [48] is of the opinion that six or eight people acquainted with the situation suffice to render the knowledge public property. Here however canonical equity (Canon 20) will permit an increasing of the number since this is certainly a *res odiosa* to the mother. Blat [49] admits the knowledge, actual or virtual, concerning the woman's illegitimate child-bearing suffices to constitute a public fact though the child in question is not precisely the cause of the knowledge. The whole matter, indeed, hinges upon relativities and no conclusion more helpful may be arrived at than this dictum *"Quia res facti est, in aestimatione boni viri esse debet."* [50]

Concerning the inscription of the mother's name, the second category is more easily handled. If for any reason the mother asks in writing that her name be entered as such in the record her wish is generally acceded to. It must be noted that the word generally is important since, as shall be seen almost immediately, exceptions to this rule may happen. When the petition is made before two witnesses, godparents for example, the inscription likewise is to be made. In such cases, however, one must be certain that the mother herself, no other person, freely, neither through force nor fear, offers her name for inscribing.[51] To sum up, therefore, it can be said that when there is no question of public maternity the baptismal inscription of the mother's name depends upon the course of action elected by her.

Vermeersch-Creusen having in purpose the prevention of every occasion of infamy qualified the nórm of procedure in cases where the maternal petition, written or oral, has been made.[52] Adulterine and incestuous children are not to be given in writing the names of

[47] Vermeersch-Creusen, *Epitome,* III, n. 379; Ayrinhac, *Penal Legislation,* p. 29; Bouuaert-Simenon, *Manuale,* n. 1241.

[48] *Epitome,* III, n. 384, 3.

[49] *Commentarium,* III, n. 68.

[50] D'Annibale, Summula, I, n. 242 (note 49).

[51] Blat, *Commentarium,* III, n. 68.

[52] Epitóme, II, n. 55.

their parents,[53] when they are not known as such. Hence even in the case of a married woman who declares said child to be adulterine and her husband denies his paternity, the child must be recorded as the legitimate offspring, unless evident arguments to the contrary are adduced as Canon 1115 declares. Even where the notation will add no infamy, as in the case of the progeny of a civil adulterous marriage, fear of scandal should deter one from inscribing until the Ordinary has been consulted. Some cases, too, admit of recourse to the Sacred Congregation of Council for a manner of proceeding.[54]

In general the same ideas prevail when there is question of inscribing the name of the father. A letter to the pastor from the male progenitor acknowledging his relationship to the child will suffice to record him as such.[55] Acknowledgment before witnesses is equally acceptable and this should be put in writing. Between the mother and child a natural bond exists and this is employed as the basis of the first principle of the law on inscription in her case. The same is not true of the father hence the law attempts to equalize the burden by recognizing a legal bond between the father and child, *i. e.*, a public authentic document proving his paternity. Such a document may be ecclesiastical or civil [56] but care must be taken that it is public and authentic, not merely private.[57] An example in point, particularly a common civil document, is an order by the court whereby the reputed father is forced to contribute to the support of the child. In such a case as this evidently no infamy will result from the inscription.[58] Such documents are to be saved, or at least the recording number registered, as proof and for one's own safety. If witnesses to verbal recognition are used enter them as such. Ordinarily, one can number such a document and paste it in the back of

[53] Hence applicable to inscription of father's name as well.

[54] *Com Ad. C. C. auth. Interp.*, July 14, 1922, ad VIII—*A. A. S.*, XIV (1922), 528.

[55] Blat, *Commentarium*, III, n. 68.

[56] Cappello, *De Sacramentis*, I, n. 188, 5. Canon 1813, § 1, categorizes ecclesiastical documents; civil documents will draw their characteristics from the laws of the place.

[57] Blat, *Commentarium*, III, n. 68.

[58] Blat, *ibid.*

the register since the cases are few, then in the register itself refer to pasted document. The file index system also may be used.

In conclusion, it must be stated that, because of the failure of such circumstances to be verified in most actual cases of illegitimacy, the pastor will generally be limited to the simple inscription *patre ignoto*. When both the name of the mother and that of the father have been entered, the status of the child is not to be noted by the word "illegitimate" but some term such as *ex matrimonio civili* or *extra matr. nat.* because of civil effects, should be employed.

The final consideration in this matter of parental inscription deals with a group of the baptized, the issue of what the Code of Canon Law calls the marriage of conscience.[59] The secrecy which surrounds such a marriage ceremony necessitates an equal caution against publicity when it is a question of the children's baptism.

This section of matrimonial legislation owes its origin to Pope Benedict XIV [60] and the method of procedure he devised is embodied totally in the Code.[61] At this time only the regulations on the inscription in connection with baptism are of interest. In No. 11 of the Papal document [62] it is directed that the child be baptized in the church no differently from other children. The real name must be given [63] else the parochial record of baptism would lack any character of a real record, the entirety would be false. However the names of the parents are to be withheld or false names given. Upon the completion of this performance, the father or the mother, if he has since died, is held to report immediately to the Ordinary of the place where the marriage was celebrated, by letter or through a worthy person (the minister of the baptism or him who celebrated the marriage), the fact of baptism, giving the place, the time and stating whether the names of the parents were withheld or false names employed. If the Ordinary is not so informed within thirty days, when the child

[59] Canons 1104-1107.

[60] Ep. encycl., *Satis Vobis,* November 17, 1741—*Fontes,* n. 319.

[61] Canons 1104-1107.

[62] *Supra;* Blat, *Commentarium,* III, n. 512-513; Payen, *De Matrimonio,* II, n. 1942, pp. 4, 5.

[63] Augustine, *Commentary,* V, 317; *Satis Vobis,* No. 12, lends an argument *ex silentio* for the support of this opinion.

has been born, baptized and the parents' names suppressed, as a penalty the marriage and birth are to be divulged.[64] It is the duty of the priest assisting at such a marriage to acquaint the parties with this rule of action and its sanction in the event that the union prove fruitful.[65]

The information forwarded to the Ordinary, including the parents' true names, is to be entered in a special book. This record, to be opened only for registration [66] and though distinct from the peculiar register of marriages, is to be kept with the same diligence in the secret archives of the bishop.[67] This register, also, has a value in the matter of proof equal to that of the parochial books and certificates drawn from it are to be accorded recognition as of full force and credence.[68] Once the marriage of conscience has been divulged this procedure does not hold for the baptism of later children. Circumstances must decide whether or not the records of those previously born are to become parochial.

Article II

Subsequent Annotations of the Baptismal Register

1. *Annotation of Confirmation*

This particular piece of legislation [69] had no existence prior to the Code. Also the law on the inscription of the confirmed from its inception underwent little, if any, change, hence the Code and its commentators merely direct that the fact of confirmation should be noted in the baptismal record.[70] Obviously, therefore, it will suffice to re-

[64] Ep. encycl., *Satis Vobis*, No. 12.

[65] Ep. encycl., *Satis Vobis*, No. 13.

[66] Augustine, *Commentary*, V, p. 318.

[67] Canon 379.

[68] *Satis Vobis*, No. 14.

[69] " . . . *praeter adnotationem in libro baptizatorum de qua in Canon 470, § 2.*"

[70] Canons 470, § 2; Blat, *Commentarium*, III, 96; Cappello, *De Sacramentis*, I, n. 221, 3.

late for registration in the parochial book of baptism just such things as prove conclusively the reception of the Sacrament of Confirmation. The name of the confirmed, the place and the date of the administration will encompass the requirements of the law.[71]

The obligation of the pastor of baptism in this regard gives rise to a reciprocal and previous obligation on the part of the minister of the Sacrament. Ordinarily he will delegate some one (pastor of the confirmed) to care for such matters. The latter is held to notify the pastor of baptism concerning the fact that the one baptized has now been confirmed.[72] Cocchi includes the subject as an alternate held to bring such information to the pastor,[73] but this is not easily conceived of in confirmation, though it has place in some cases of marriage.[74]

Canon 799 declares that one other than the minister may inform, and usually does, the proper pastor of the confirmed when he has not been present at the ceremony. In like manner, the pastor of baptism may be made cognizant of the administration of this, the second Sacrament received.[75] Hence occasions may arise when the minister of the Sacrament in person or through another has to notify two pastors, one of the confirmation, the other of the baptism, concerning the fact that the Sacrament of Confirmation has been conferred. Ordinarily the pastor of the confirmed will pass on such information by means of an authentic document to the pastor of baptism.

2. *Matrimonial Annotation*

Canon 1103, § 2. Praeterea, ad normam Canon 470, § 2, parochus in libro quoque baptizatorum adnotet conjugem tali die in sua paroecia matrimonium contraxisse. Quod si conjux alibi baptizatus fuerit, matrimonii parochus notitiam initi contractus ad parochum baptismi sive per se sive per curiam episcopalem transmittat, ut matrimonium in baptizatorum librum referatur.

71 Vromant, *Jus Missionariorum,* II, n. 335.
72 De Meester, *Juris Canonici,* I, II, n. 859, a.
73 *Commentarium,* II, III, n. 350.
74 Canon 1103, § 3.
75 Fanfani, *De Jure Parochorum,* n. 244, C. a.

From the viewpoint of time the legislation embodied in Canon 1103, § 2, appears to antedate the Code of Canon Law,[76] yet in truth it is part and parcel of that codification. In importance, this is an outstanding development in the parochial books since the two principal registers are brought into a closer relation and the desire of the Fathers of the Council of Trent, to make the baptismal register an aid to the celebration of valid marriages,[77] is satisfied.

The practical value of the matrimonial addition to the baptismal register is evident. The existence of the impediment of the bond, affinity, etc., is thereby rendered much more easy to detect,[78] and anything which is of aid to determine the free state of persons in these days is appreciable.

The record of baptism, therefore, is required to be, among other things, a brief matrimonial register. To the record of the person baptized at a given place and duly entered as such the chief circumstances of his or her marriage are to be added.[79] If one or both parties to the marriage have been baptized in the church of the marriage the pastor adds to the records of baptism, the name of the one with whom marriage was contracted, the date and the place of celebration.[80] Often, however, it will be necessary for the assisting pastor or licensed priest to inform another pastor or other pastors concerning the facts of the marriage.[81]

The content of such an informing notice has been set forth in an instruction emanating from the Sacred Congregation of Sacraments in 1921.[82] Herein the pastor of celebration is required (and the

[76] S. C. C., *Ne Temere,* August 2, 1907—*A. S. S.*, XL (1907), 529. For all intents and purposes this is the same as the legislation of the Code, save for a few very detailed points.

[77] Pallavicino, *Istoria del Concilio di Trento*, IV, 594.

[78] Cappello, *De Sacramentis,* III, n. 719, 1.

[79] Canon 1103, § 2.

[80] Blat, *Commentarium,* III, n. 506.

[81] In mixed marriages the baptismal pastor of the Catholic party alone is notified. Cappello, *De Sacramentis,* III, n. 719.

When the place of baptism is situated in Russia, this and all other notices are sent to the Pontifical Commission for Russia. *S. C. pro Ecclesia Orientali,* July 13, 1928—*A. A. S.*, XX (1928), 260.

[82] July 4, 1921—*A. A. S.*, XIII (1921), 349.

other pastor can demand it) to transmit without voluntary delay the names and surnames of the parties and their parents, the ages of the spouses, the place and date of the marriage, the names and surnames of the witnesses. Finally, the pastor adds his name and stamps the document with the parochial seal. The Congregation in the same place demands the securance and use of all information possible as an aid to the safe conveyance of this knowledge to its destination. If the place of baptism is unknown generally the diocese of origin can be presumed from the place of birth, hence transfer will then be made to the supposed Ordinary of origin.[83]

In regard to the transmission, the Code allows the pastor himself to perform this act or it may be carried out by the episcopal curia. The instruction of the Congregation of Sacraments, too, sees in the curial transference a much safer means.[84] Above all, the Congregation stressed the necessity of the transmission calling upon the Ordinaries to punish those who neglect this and other matters dealing with inscription of the registers.[85] Previously, a like mind had been manifested when the same Congregation refused to dispense from the annotation of the baptismal register unless such additions were morally impossible.[86]

Whether the marriage has been celebrated according to the ordinary canonical form [87] or in what the authors term the extraordinary form,[88] the regulations concerning transmission obtain.[89] The latter class of marriages must therefore receive attention, as well as those of the ordinary form already seen.

Canon 1098 includes two categories. In the first a priest is present, while in the second this witness is absent. When a priest is present, though neither pastor nor his delegate, he assists at the marriage and is held to transmit the necessary information to the pastors

[83] *Wouters, De Forma Promissionis et Celebrationis Matrimonii*, p. 67.

[84] S. C. de Sacr., July 4, 1921—*A. A. S.*, XIII (1921), 349; Capello, *De Sacramentis*, III, n. 719, 2, c.

[85] *Op cit.*, ns. 3, 6.

[86] S. C. de Sacr., March 13, 1910—*A. A. S.*, II (1910), 193; Augustine, *Commentary*, V, 313.

[87] Canons 1094-1097.

[88] Canon 1098.

[89] Canon 1103, § 2, § 3.

of baptism.[90] In such a case, some authors place the onus of transmission upon the priest alone,[91] while others include the contracting parties.[92] The first opinion seems preferable since the text of the Canon rather indicates the priest's sole obligation. Also the restriction of responsibility would dictate the same. In the event that no priest assisted responsibility for the transmission rests as an obligation *in solidum* upon the parties and the witnesses, that is, all are equally bound until one performs the required action.[93] The fulfillment of this duty may be sufficiently achieved either by letter or by personal appearance before the pastor.[94]

It would appear that in both of these cases the responsible persons are held not only to notify the pastor having the matrimonial jurisdiction but also the pastor or pastors of baptism.[95] However, a probable opinion exists for the notification of the proper pastor of the marriage and allowing him to make the second transmission, namely, to the pastor maintaining the baptismal record.[96] Should he refuse, the minister or the parties and witnesses, if there is no minister, are held. Similar circumstances in baptism see a like procedure commonly followed, hence why not here as well.[97] If through this action it is discovered that one of the parties in this or any other case is in some way dirimently impeded from contracting marriage, the receiving pastor immediately informs to that effect the pastor who had the right to assist at the celebration of the marriage.[98]

Later, the question of the registration of dispensations shall be

[90] Canon, 1103, § 3 . . . *ut adnotetur in praescriptis libris,* means the matrimonial and baptismal registers.

[91] Cappello, *De Sacramentis,* III, n. 720, 2; Blat, *Commentarium,* III, n. 506; Payen, *De Matrimonio,* II, n. 1924.

[92] Augustine, *Commentary,* V, 314; Wouters, *De Forma,* p. 67; Wernz-Vidal, *Jus Canonicum,* V, n. 563.

[93] Cappello, *De Sacramentis,* III, n. 720, 3; Augustine, *A Commentary,* V, 214.

[94] Blat, *Commentarium,* III, 506; Payen, *De Matrimonio,* II, n. 1922, note 3.

[95] Cappello, *De Sacramentis,* III, 720, 3.

[96] Payen, *De Matrimonio,* II, 1922; De Smet, *Betrothment and Marriage,* II, 214, B (foot note).

[97] Fanfani, *De Jure Parochorum,* n. 244, D.

[98] S. C. de Sacr., July 4, 1921—n. 5, *A. A. S.,* XIII (1921), 349.

treated. Here, however, it is proper to deal with the inscription of the dispensation from the form of marriage since such a dispensation affects the marriage to the extent of rendering it a marriage in the extraordinary form. It is stated in Canon 1046 that a dispensation given in the external forum for such a marriage as Canon 1044 visualizes, which includes marriages in the extraordinary form [99] must be recorded in the register of marriage. From this it follows that such a marriage ought to be entered, as an annotation, in the baptismal record.[100]

Now marriages performed by reason of Canon 1044 divide themselves into two classes. The first comprises those capable of entrance in the parochial register of matrimony, and the second those similar in this respect to marriages of conscience and occultly convalidated marriages,[101] that is, the record of their celebration belongs in the curial archives for both the matrimonial registration and the matrimonial annotation of the baptismal record.[102]

Canon 1046 restricts the act of registration to matters of the external forum, hence when there is question of a public impediment.[103] This is the reason why no such obligation is imposed upon the pastor employing similarly extensive powers by virtue of Canon 1045 since said Canon expressly limits the dispensing power to occult cases; otherwise a conflict would arise with Canon 1757, § 3, 2°. Therefore it is evident that the pastor acting with the power granted him in Canon 1044 is held to inscribe only those marriages wherein a public impediment exists. Hence he needs transmit the notice of such a marriage to the pastor or pastors of baptism or better to see that the diocesan curia takes care of this transference.[104] This obligation it must be remembered does not exist if the impediment though public in itself is not such in fact.[105]

[99] Canon 1043, " . . . *tum super forma in matrimonii celebratione servanda* . . . "

[100] Blat, *Commentarium,* III, n. 438.

[101] Payen, *De Matrimonio,* II, n. 2566, 1.

[102] Wernz-Vidal, *Jus Canonicum,* V, n. 428.

[103] Blat, *Commentarium,* III, n. 438; Cappello, *De Sacramentis,* III, n. 241.

[104] Blat, *ibid.*

[105] Blat, *ibid.*

Neither the legislation for the ordinary form of marriage nor that for the extraordinary form includes a class of marriages which must be considered here because they are excepted from inscription in the parochial book of baptism. These are marriages of conscience which have been reviewed previously from a different angle. The necessary secrecy that enshrouds them prevents their inclusion in the ordinary baptismal register of a parish just as the parochial book of marriage lacks their entry.[106] The book preserved in the secret archives of the curia in consonance with Canon 379 receives the baptismal registration of these marriages.

Then there is the question of just what influence, if any, will be had upon the baptismal register in the event a marriage has been convalidated. If such a marriage has had the *species vel figura matrimonii* the proper records will already exist by reason by Canons 1103 and 470, § 2. All that is needed then is an addition to the register of marriage indicating its convalidation providing the nullity arose from a public impediment.[107] Should the nullity arise from an occult cause the parochial record is ignored and the secret book of the episcopal curia utilized.[108] Nothing of these matters will appear in the baptismal register. However if the marriage in question has never been properly entered in accordance with Canon 1103 then the regulation must be carried out and the proper inscriptions made, yet in consonance with the foregoing norm concerning the occultness or publicity of the invalid marriage. Said criterion will indicate wherein the marriage is to be recorded. Following this decision for the matrimonial inscription, the parochial baptismal register or the special register is annotated not, however, because of the convalidation but in view of the prescription of Canon 470, § 2.

Another development from marriage does have a direct bearing upon the matrimonial annotation in the record of baptisms. When a previously registered marriage has been declared null whether by

[106] Payen, *De Matrimonio,* II, n. 1928; Canon 1107.

[107] Vlaming, *De Matrimonio,* II, n. 771; Payen, *De Matrimonio,* II, n. 2566, No. 2; Gasparri, *De Matrimonio,* II, n. 1281.

[108] Payen, *De Matrimonio,* II, n. 2566, 1; Gasparri, *De Matrimonio,* II, n. 1400.

the judicial process [109] or by the procedure envisioned in Canon 1990, or in cases of a dispensation ***super ratum et nonconsummatum*** and religious profession [110] the baptismal register must be amended to show the proper status of the persons after such an action. Accordingly, Canon 1988 directs that both the matrimonial and the baptismal registers be annotated to show that the putative spouses are free from the supposed bond of marriage. The same Canon declares that the Ordinary is obliged to see that notice to this effect be sent to the proper pastor or pastors, which transmission may be made through the Curia, by the Ordinary himself or by one directed by him to do so.[111] Finally the annotation of the baptismal register to show that marriage has been contracted by virtue of the Pauline Privilege will be a distinct safeguard against future questioning concerning the previous marriage.

3. *Annotations of Holy Orders and Solemn Religious Profession*

Canon 1011. Praeterea loci Ordinarius, si agatur de ordinatis e clero saeculari, aut Superior major, si de religiosis ordinatis cum suis litteris dimissoriis, notitiam celebratae ordinationis uniuscuiusque subdiaconi transmittat ad parochum baptismi, qui id adnotet in suo baptizatorum libro ad norman Canon 470, § 2.

Canon 576, § 2. . . . si agatur de professione solemni, Superior eam excipiens debet profitentis parochum baptismi de eadem certiorem reddere, ad norman Canon 470, § 2.

The final regulations of Canon 470, § 2, on the subsequent inscriptions of the baptismal register direct that the reception of subdeaconship and solemn religious profession must be recorded in the baptismal register. The complement of this prescription is found in

[109] Canon 1988.

[110] Canon 1119; S. C. de Sacr., May 7, 1923, n. 106—*A. A. S.*, XV (1923), 413, directs the Ordinary to command the pastors concerned to annotate the proper books, those of marriage and of baptism.

[111] Blat, *Commentarium,* IV, n. 522.

Canon 1011 for subdeaconship and Canon 576, § 2, for the profession. The purpose of the law in introducing such measures again is founded in the matter of free status for entrance into marriage, which status is radically affected by the above designated acts [112] both rendering any attempt at marriage invalid.[113] If later a dispensation, not obtained in the sacramental forum, regains for such a person the freedom to marry this must be noted in the baptismal register.

Concerning subdeaconship the law directs the transference of the information regarding the entrance into Holy Orders to the pastor of baptism.[114] In commenting upon this it may well be noted first that this notification is needed only for subdeaconship, higher orders are not included.[115] Just what will constitute the sum and substance of this transmission for entrance into the record of baptism authors fail to say. The paucity of information required to be entered in what Augustine terms the "roster of the ordained" [116] makes it necessary to transfer the entirety to the pastor of baptism. Hence, the notification is to contain the name of the ordained, that of the ordaining minister, the date and the place of ordination.[117]

Canon 1011 makes it incumbent upon two classes of superiors to fulfill this obligation of transmission. The Ordinary of the place, whether he ordained or permitted another to do so, is responsible for the carrying out of this prescription for his own subjects.[118] When it is a question of religious, however, a distinction must be made. Major superiors of religious ordained wth dimissorials from them must effect this transfer. Hence this class is composed of the major superiors of exempt religious since no others can give dimissorials for the reception of Sacred Orders [119] unless a special indult is had by non-exempt religious or even societies without vows in which case their superiors enjoy this same competence. On the other hand, religious

[112] Cocchi, *Commentarium,* II, n. 350, A, d; Augustine, *A Commentary,* II, 557.

[113] Canons 1072, 1073.

[114] Canons 1011, 470, § 2.

[115] Blat, *Commentarium,* III, n. 394.

[116] *A Commentary,* IV, p. 548.

[117] Augustine, *A Commentary,* IV, p. 548; Blat, *Commentarium,* III, n. 393.

[118] Blat, *op. cit.,* III, n. 394.

[119] Canon 964, 2°; Augustine, *A Commentary,* IV, 549.

who come into major orders *jure saecularium*,[120] place no responsibility in this matter upon their superiors. The onus falls upon the Ordinary of the place where the religious house to which the ordained belong is situated.[121]

As is usual in the conducting of such affairs the Ordinary or the responsible religious superior attends to the matter through a personal delegate or one *ex officio* constituted to care for such affairs, *e. g.*, the Chancellor. The transmission, however, though made through private letter by one other than he who is canonically preferred or delegated must be given under the signature of the Ordinary of the place or the religious superior.[122]

Though subdeaconship has been received and the baptismal record annotated to that effect yet the reception of solemn profession, if made, must likewise be inscribed in the same register because diverse laws direct thus (Canons 1011, 576, § 2) and legally diverse impediments arise (Canons 1072, 1073).[123] The simple perpetual profession of the Jesuits by reason of a special prescription of the Holy See[124] is likewise included in this regulation, as Canon 1073 clearly shows.

As to the transmission of this information, he who receives the profession should forward the necessary notification to the interested pastor for inscription but he may delegate another to act in his place yet it must be done in the name of the former[125] and in such a way as he thinks sufficient to render the notification certain.[126] This notification ought to contain the name of the professed, in what Order, who received him, the place (province, abbey) and date. All this may be drawn from the record of profession kept by the institute and this much will suffice to satisfy the demands of the law.

120 Canon 964, 4°.

121 Canon 965, Blat, *Commentarium,* III, n. 394.

122 Blat, *ibid.*

123 Schäfer, *De Religiosis,* n. 281, 4.

124 Const., *Ascendente Domino,* Gregory XIII, May 25, 1584, n. 22—*Fontes,* n. 153.

125 Schäfer, *De Religiosis,* n. 281, 4.

126 Blat, *Commentarium,* II, n. 647.

ARTICLE III

CERTIFICATES, BAPTISMAL AND OTHERWISE

Practically, the certificate of baptism is to be more or less a replica of the registration itself. The nature of the certificates was under discussion elsewhere [127] hence it will not be necessary to cover the entire field again. A few points, however, merit special consideration here.

The certificate is nothing more than a convenient form for the exhibition of information contained in the parochial book. With regard to the baptismal certificate the Code apparently directs that each certificate issued should contain a record of all the subsequent annotations which have been placed in the register of the baptized.[128] This appears, upon occasion, to be a rather useless procedure and unless it is a question of marriage or the request for the inclusion of the additions is made one may omit the annotations from the certificate of baptism.[129] At first glance, this insinuates a contradiction to the explicit prescription of the Code, yet it is not so if consideration is given to the fact that these additions, save for that of confirmation, bear directly upon matrimony and are construed as such by the various authors cited throughout the chapter. Hence, given a case where the baptismal certificate is to play no part in the canonical preparation for marriage, the annotations may rightly be omitted from the certificate.

What has been said here concerning the baptismal attestation applies with the necessary modifications to the other certificates. Since none of these are of very great moment by reason of divergencies from the baptismal certificate, it will not be necessary to consider each with its proper book. The major point made here in the question of certificates, the annotations, is not moved in the other registers, except in that of matrimony. In the case of that register such annotations as affect the status of the parties to a marriage, declaration of nullity, dissolution or convalidation, are to be entered in the certificate in the event that the parochial book of marriage is thus inscribed.

[127] Chapter I, pp. 11-13.

[128] Canon 470, § 2.

[129] Augustine, *A Commentary,* II, 557.

CHAPTER V

THE MATRIMONIAL REGISTER

THE most important points of discussion concerning the registration of marriages deal more extensively with where this record is to be placed rather than what shall comprise the same. Certainly, the ordinary contents of this register, the names of the contracting parties, parents and witnesses, together with the place and date of the celebration are important, however, the major problems of matrimonial inscription are not centered upon these matters. Other potential elements of the matrimonial contract merit the greater amount of consideration from the authors.

With this in mind, therefore, the subject matter here is seen to divide itself into, first, a consideration of the inscription of a marriage following the ordinary form,[1] next, of a marriage celebrated in the extraordinary form,[2] then the registration of marriages of conscience [3] and finally, consideration is given some accidental additions which may adhere to any of the foregoing classifications.

ARTICLE I

REGISTRATION OF MARRIAGES OF THE ORDINARY FORM

Canon 1103, § 1. Celebrato matrimonio, parochus vel qui ejus vices gerit, quamprimum describat in libro matrimoniorum nomina conjugum ac testium, locum et diem celebrati matrimonii atque alia secundum modum in libris ritualibus et a proprio Ordinario praescriptum; idque licet alius Sacerdos vel a se vel ab Ordinario delegatus matrimonio adstiterit.

[1] Canons 1094-1097.

[2] Canon 1098.

[3] Canons 1104-1106.

§ 2. Praeterea, ad normam Canon 470, § 2, parochus in libro quoque baptizatorum adnotet conjugem tali die in sua paroecia matrimonium contraxisse. Quod si conjux alibi baptizatus fuerit, matrimonii parochus notitiam initi contractus ad parochum baptismi sive per sive per curiam episcopalem transmittat, ut matrimonium in baptizatorum librum referatur.

1. *The Inscriber*

In consonance with the general norms of registration, the onus of inscription falls most properly upon the pastor of the parties to the marriage,[4] as the above Canon clearly demonstrates. However, it must be recalled here that any pastor within his parish limits can validly assist at the marriage of anyone, even that of nonsubjects.[5] Hence, though his assistance is illicit if permission or a just cause is lacking still he had the obligation to record the marriage in his parochial book of matrimony.[6]

The legislator in formulating § 1 of the above quoted Canon has seen fit to include the clause "... *qui ejus vices gerit* ...," an alternative which appears in no other canonical regulation for the inscription of the parochial books. Elsewhere, the minister is given canonical recognition but with qualification. His inscription must be subsigned by the pastor.[7] Here that is not necessary, the vice-gerent is unqualifiedly empowered to draw up the record. Who then receive the recognition accorded by § 1 of Canon 1103?

The general norms dealing with persons introduce to this class such as the econome, the substitute pastor, the adjutor and the quasi-pastor,[8] because they possess equal rights with the pastor. After assisting at the celebration of a marriage these are obliged to inscribe the marriage in the proper register and to sign it with their own

[4] Canon 1097.

[5] Canon 1095, § 1, 2°.

[6] Vlaming, *Praelectiones,* II, n. 603; Cappello, *De Sacramentis,* III, n. 718, 1.

[7] Cappello, *De Sacramentis,* III, 767-768; Vermeersch-Creusen, *Epitome,* II, 28.

[8] Canons 451, 471-475; Payen, *De Matrimonio,* II, n. 1909, 2.

names.[9] This power so exercised, however, is not limited to marriage alone, they are equally recognized by the law when it is a question of the inscription of any of the parochial books, hence one must look elsewhere for an extraordinary application of this term.

As has been seen before [10] the Code does not endow more probably the curate or assistant (*vicarius cooperator*) with any general power in the matter of inscribing the parochial registers. But when the question of the matrimonial inscription arises there is a possibility of his acquiring said faculty though he continue to lack the right to make other registrations. By reason of the exception for general delegation found in Canon 1096, § 1, the curate or assistant may become a pastor *quoad matrimonium* either through episcopal designation or by delegation of the pastor.[11] The pastoral right thus obtained brings to the assistant a corresponding duty to care for the inscriptions to be made in the parochial record of marriage and under his own name. Finally, it is well to bear in mind here that the minister whether he be the Ordinary, the pastor or vice-gerent when celebrating a marriage of his subjects outside his own territory or any priest delegated to assist at a marriage is not held to the performance of the inscription.[12] The pastor of the place is required to inscribe the record of the marriage in the proper register.

Within what time is the pastor required to make this inscription? The decree *Ne Temere* [13] speaking on this point said *statim*,[14] however the Code has amended this to *quamprimum*, a term of somewhat less urgency.[15] Numerically this is ordinarily not to be placed beyond three or four days.[16] Other authors, more properly it seems, interpret it as excluding negligence and the proximate possibility of

[9] Augustine, *A Commentary*, V, 312.

[10] Chapter I, pp. 15, 16.

[11] Among other places, in the Archdiocese of Philadelphia the Ordinary has given such delegation to assistants.

[12] Cappello, *De Sacramentis*, III, 718; Payen, *De Matrimonio*, II, 1909, 1.

to inscribe the record of the marriage in the proper register.

[13] S. C. de Sacr., August 2, 1907—*A. S. S.* (1907) XL, p. 529.

[14] Vlaming proposes this now. *Praelectiones*, II, 603.

[15] Payen, *De Matrimonio*, II, n. 1910, 1.

[16] Gasparri, *De Matrimonio*, II, n. 1075.

forgetting the registration.[17] To prevent such a happening it is suggested that the register be placed in the sacristy for registration immediately after the ceremony [18] thereby obviating the use of another book or a sheet of paper as a temporary record.[19]

2. *Contents of the Inscription*

Canon 1103, § 1, in enumerating what should constitute the record of a marriage explicitly demands several things and in addition leaves the way open for further entries by a general admonition to the pastor that he supply also such information as the Ritual and prescriptions of his proper Ordinary demand.

The definitely required information of the Code includes only those things that are absolutely necessary to constitute a really authentic ecclesiastical document of marriage and involves no disputable matter. The names of the parties to the marriage are obviously essential. The names of the witnesses, both the qualified [20] and the ordinary, must be included. The place and the date [21] distinguish the marriage further and render the record authentic and complete. One should have a care that the date on the return portion of the civil license coincides with that placed in the register. In connection with this one should be warned against antedating marriages. Beyond these few words of purpose nothing remains to be said for the explicit canonical requirements in regard to the registration of marriage.

The possibilities inherent in the regulation concerning the ritual and episcopal prescriptions are much greater. The latter of these two sources may be neglected since conditions peculiar to a given place will prompt extraordinary measures of the Ordinary, while the usual additional requisites are covered by the Ritual.

In Title XII, Chapter IV, the Roman Ritual treats of the matter of matrimonial inscription. To the requirements of Canon 1103 ad-

[17] Blat, *Commentarium,* III, n. 506; Augustine, *A Commentary,* V, 312.

[18] Gasparri, *ibid.*

[19] Vlaming, *Praelectiones,* II, n. 603, note 5.

[20] Cappello, *De Sacramentis,* III, n. 649; Payen, *De Matrimonio,* II, n. 1911, 1.

[21] Year, month and day to be written out; Payen, *De Matrimonio,* II, n. 1911; Wouters, *Form of Marriage*. p. 65.

ditions are made.[22] The first of these demands the recording of the publishing of the banns, particularly in the event that they were published elsewhere, also omission of one or more should be noted.[23] The names of the parents, the age and the parish of the spouses, the parochial residence of the witnesses all are required. The fact that consent was asked and received, the nuptial blessing was given, are recommended for inclusion. When a widow or widower is a party to the marriage the name of the deceased spouse is recorded. Finally, the status of the qualified witness, whether he assisted by virtue of his ordinary power or by reason of express permission, is to be set down. These are the practical additions made by the Roman Ritual to the canonical regulations for the inscription of a marriage and since they cover a rather extensive field, though of no great difficulty, it is fitting in conclusion to recall the cardinal principle, as it were, of all registration that anything capable of injuring or defaming the parties is to be omitted.[24]

3. *Transmission of Marriage Notification*

This matter has been seen already when treatment was accorded the matrimonial annotation of the baptismal register. Here a slight repetition is made to emphasize the fact that the pastor of the place of marriage has a double obligation dealing with the inscription of a marriage if one or both parties to the same were baptized elsewhere. Beside his duty to inscribe the marriage in its proper register he is held to notify in detail the pastor or pastors of baptism concerning the fact of marriage.[25] This he may do himself or through the agency of the diocesan Curia.[26] In the event that he is the pastor of baptism as well, there is no need of notification. Immediately he performs the proper annotation.[27]

[22] *Rit. Roman.*, p. 509 ss.

[23] P. 510.

[24] Gasparri, *De Matrimonio*, II, n. 1281 (3rd ed.); Payen, *De Matrimonio*, II, 1912, 2.

[25] Payen, *De Matrimonio*, II, n. 1914.

[26] Canon 1103, § 2.

[27] Payen, *De Matrimonio*, II, n. 1915.

Article II

Registration of Marriages Celebrated in the Extraordinary Form

Canon 1103, § 3. Quoties matrimonium ad normam Canon 1098 contrahitur, sacerdos, si eidem adstiterit, secus testes tenentur in solidum cum contrahentibus curare ut initum conjugium in praescriptis libris quamprimum adnotetur.

The Code, being as inclusive as possible in its matrimonial legislation, has visualized cases wherein grave reason will demand the celebration of marriage in a mode other than the ordinary canonical form. The author has in purpose here a treatment of the inscription to be made in such cases.

The question of content can be dismissed without further notice. The treatment lately accorded that question suffices for this also since the differentiating qualities, from the viewpoint of inscription, of the two do not bear upon this matter. Rather, the surrounding circumstances are chiefly responsible for a scrutiny of marriages performed according to Canon 1098, that a canonical mode of inscriptional procedure may be laid down in accordance with Canon 1103, § 3.

The extraordinary form of marriage finds its usual employment in the circumstances surrounding a deathbed marriage or a marriage celebrated in a place where it is prudently foreseen that a month will pass before the Ordinary, pastor or a delegated priest will come or will be able to be reached. It must be remembered, too, that the nonaccessibility of a priest must be present in a deathbed marriage as well as in the other case.[28] Given these canonical circumstances the law declares that a valid and licit union will be effected if witnesses are present. No. 2, however, adds a qualification stating that if any priest may be had then the marriage ought to be witnessed by him together with the others.

[28] Canon 1098, 1°, 2°.

Canon 1103, § 3 in a general way considers the registration of this species of marriage. If a priest is present it is his obligation to see that the marriage is recorded.[29] Otherwise the contracting parties and the witnesses have an obligation *in solidum* to effect the regular inscription in the parochial book of matrimony.[30] A partial treatment of this question was given when the marriage notification of the pastor of baptism was considered.[31] Now from the view of matrimonial inscription alone it is necessary to examine the situation more closely attempting to discover who is the proper pastor of such a marriage, that is, to whom is the priest or are the parties and witnesses to convey the information demanded by Canon 1103, § 1.

The possibilities of such a situation bring two pastors into its ambit, the pastor of the place of marriage and the pastor who in the ordinary course of events ought to have been the official witness of the Church, the domicilar pastor of the parties or at least of the woman. Payen [32] prudently admits that in view of controversy liberty obtains, hence one may choose to notify the pastor of the place or the proper pastor. In practise, declares Cappello,[33] transmit the information to the pastor of the place where the marriage was performed. This opinion can be said to serve some support from Vlaming's assertion [34] that the pastor of the place should make the record though he illicitly assisted at the marriage. Also, it appears that the opinion supporting the notification of the pastor of the domicile bears too much upon the old law as found in the decree *Tametsi.*[35] Finally, if the marriage was performed in a place where there is no parish or quasi-parish the report goes to the Ordinary of the place.[36]

At times, the marriage visualized in Canon 1098, particularly the deathbed marriage, will require inscription in the secret matrimonial register of the curial archives to save the fame of the persons con-

[29] Cappello, *De Sacramentis,* III, n. 720, 2; Blat, *Commentarium,* III, n. 506; Payen, *De Matrimonio,* II, n. 1924, note.

[30] Cappello, *op cit.,* n. 720, 3; Augustine, *A Commentary,* V, p. 214.

[31] Chapter IV, article II.

[32] *De Matrimonio,* II, n. 1922.

[33] *De Sacramentis,* III, n. 720, 3.

[34] *Praelectiones,* II, n. 603, note 2.

[35] Payen, *De Matrimonio,* II, n. 1916, 3.

[36] Wouters, *De Forma,* p. 67, III, 2, note.

cerned and yet give proof of the legitimacy of the children.[37] This, too, is the proper procedure for inscribing what is known as *matrimonium jurejurando probatum*. Such a marriage is had when persons unable to show legitimate proof of their marriage in some distant place are accepted upon their oath as legitimately married and the children of them legitimate. To have proof of such a marriage a record of it is made in the special book[38] in custody of the Curia.[39]

Article III

Registration of Marriages of Conscience

Canon 1107. Matrimonium conscientiae non est adnotandum in consueto matrimoniorum ac baptizatorum libro, sed in peculiari libro servando in secreto Curiae archivo de quo in Canon 379.

Though the marriage of conscience considered from the viewpoint of its substantially constituting elements does not deviate from the ordinary form of marriage, accidentals such as the absolute secrecy surrounding its performance tend to remove it from that class. Hence, it has been given a separate place in the Code[40] and its extraordinary registration[41] fits it for special consideration, as beyond both the ordinary and extraordinary form of marriage.

The regulations of Benedict XIV,[42] that Pontiff of great canonical fame, instituted what is now known as the marriage of conscience. These same rules have been embodied in the Code under the same title[43] hence recurrence to this source of the canonical prescription aids greatly in the ascertaining of the required procedure.

The necessity of maintaining secrecy motivates the regulation of

[37] Canon 1047; Payen, *De Matrimonio*, II, n. 1929.

[38] S. C. Sacr., March 6, 1911—*A. A. S.*, III (1911), p. 103.

[39] Payen, *De Matrimonio*, II, n. 1930, 2.

[40] Canons 1104-1106.

[41] Canon 1107.

[42] Ep. encycl., *Satis Vobis*, November 17, 1741—*Fontes*, n. 319.

[43] Cappello, *De Sacramentis*, III, n. 723, 3.

this entire matrimonial affair. Causes, most grave and urgent,[44] such as iniquitous civil laws, prohibitions against marriage of civil officials,[45] must be present, which prevent a contracting of marriage in the ordinary form. Truly extraordinary must be these reasons particularly since great evils like polygamy may result from the employment of such a celebration.[46] If the Ordinary prudently judges that the required conditions are present then the marriage is performed without the publishing of banns and with all due precautions toward the maintenance of the secrecy of the union.

One of the five cautions calculated by Pope Benedict XIV to enshroud adequately the fact of the marriage was the secret recording. Canon 1107 now carries the same measure, directing the inscription, which is the same as in ordinary cases, to be made in a secret register which Canon 379 demands to be kept in the episcopal archives. Such a measure precludes the appearance of any notice concerning the marriage in the parochial book of matrimony. Likewise it prevents the transference of a marriage notification to the pastors of baptism of the parties in consonance with Canon 1103, § 2.[47] Nor may anyone have an attesting certificate, which is equal in value to that drawn from the parochial records,[48] of such a marriage unless he can prove a real right to it and demonstrate that there is no possibility of his obtaining the needed proof from another source.[49] Aside from these considerations the marriage of conscience does not affect the registration of marriages.

Article IV

Other and Accidental Inscriptions

There are yet other circumstances that may be verified in a marriage to the affecting of its inscription. Most of these concern the

[44] Canon 1104.
[45] Augustine, *A Commentary*, V, 317.
[46] Ep. encycl., *Satis Vobis*, No. 2, November 17, 1741—*Fontes*, n. 319.
[47] Augustine, *A Commentary*, V, 318.
[48] Ep. encycl., *Satis Vobis*, No. 14.
[49] Ep. encycl., *Satis Vobis*, No. 10.

status of a marriage after its performance, a few precede or accompany the same.

The Roman Ritual [50] demands that notice be given in writing in the parochial register of marriage that a dispensation has been obtained from a *de facto* public impediment, if it is such as has been dispensed from in the external forum.[51] The Code [52] placing the same qualification of publicity demands the registration even though the extraordinary form of marriage has been employed. The use of the Pauline Privilege to effect another marriage must likewise be noted in the register.

If the dispensation, on the other hand, was granted in the internal nonsacramental forum for an occult impediment the same is to be registered in the book kept in the secret archives in accord with Canon 379. By this means, in event that the impediment becomes public written proof may be produced in demonstration of its dispensation.[53]

Dispensations granted after marriage must also be inscribed. For example, the dispensation from a *ratum et non consummatum* marriage and the nullifying effect produced by solemn religious profession must be duly set down in the register.[54] Finally, even the dispensation from the banns of marriage must be noted.[55]

Marriages contracted conditionally must be taken cognizance of in the register with respect to the conditionality.[56] A convalidation of a marriage in the external forum is noted in the parochial matrimonial record.[57] Otherwise convalidated they are not entered in that book [58] but when the internal nonsacramental forum is used, then

[50] *Rit. Roman.*, XII, IV, p. 510.

[51] Genicot-Salmans, *Theologia Moralis*, II, n. 467; Augustine, *A Commentary*, V, 313; Cappello, *De Sacramentis*, III, n. 718.

[52] Canon 1046.

[53] Canon 1047; at times the Sacred Penitentiary requires the report to be made back to it. Gasparri, *De Matrimonio*, n. 406.

[54] Canon 1119; Payen, *De Matrimonio*, II, 1923; S. C. de Sacr., May 7, 1923, n. 106—*A. A. S.*, XV (1923), 413.

[55] *Rit. Roman.*, XII, IV, p. 510.

[56] Cappello, *De Sacramentis*, III, n. 625, 7.

[57] Payen, *De Matrimonio*, II, 1911, 3; Cappello, *op. cit.*, n. 718.

[58] Vlaming, *Praelectiones*, II, p. 360; Payen, *De Matrimonio*, II, n. 2566.

the register of the secret archives is utilized as a precaution against a future divulging which would involve the legitimacy of the children.

Declarations of nullity handed down either after the long judicial procedure [59] or after the Canon 1990 mode must likewise be indicated in the parochial register of marriage.[60] Such additions to the register as declaration of nullity and convalidation may be inscribed immediately with the record of the marriage or in accordance with the opinion of some authors [61] a new record is made in which reference is had clearly to the former inscription. Finally, definite and sufficient information should be sent by the Ordinary or the diocesan Curia to the pastor, in nullity cases particular attention being given to the inclusion of the date of declaration. The same holds for the one burdened with the notification concerning the convalidation of a marriage.

[59] Canon 1988.

[60] Canon 1988; Payen, *De Matrimonio,* II, n. 1911, 3; Cappello, *De Sacramentis,* III, n. 718, 8; S. C. de Sacr., May 7, 1923, n. 106—*A. A. S.*, XV (1923), p. 413.

[61] Payen, *ibid.;* Gasparri, *De Matrimonio,* II, n. 1281 (3rd ed., 1904).

CHAPTER VI

THE REMAINING REGISTERS

Article I

The Register of the Confirmed

Canon 798. Nomina ministri, confirmatorum, parentum et patrinorum, diem ac locum confirmationis parochus inscribat in peculiari libro . . .

Canon 799. Si proprius confirmati parochus praesens non fuerit, de collata confirmatione minister vel per se ipse vel per alium quamprimum eundum certiorem faciat.

Since the Sacrament of Confirmation is not able to be repeated [1] and its reception is often demanded by the Code as a qualification for certain more advanced actions in the Church it is necessary to have an authentic record from which the fact of confirmation may be proven.[2]

An inquiry into this regulation concerning inscription cannot be very extensive as the Canons themselves show. Three matters only merit attention, the content of the register, the transmission of information concerning the conferring of the Sacrament to the pastor of baptism and the notifying of the proper pastor of the confirmed in case he was not present at the administration itself.

General regulations concerning the parochial books are in force here also as is evident.[3] Specifically, the Code, in the above Canons, visualizes a separate book kept for the reception of this inscription by the pastor a record really set apart from the other registers [4] together with which it makes the group known as the parochial books.[5] A resolution of the Sacred Congregation of Council clearly states in approval of a Chapter decision that even though ancient custom has

[1] Canon 732, § 1.

[2] Blat, *Commentarium*, III, I, n. 95.

[3] Chapter I.

[4] Augustine, *A Commentary*, IV, 122.

[5] Canon 470.

established the use of one book for the inscription of the confirmed of a diocese, each pastor must maintain a parochial register of the confirmed for those subject to him by reason of Canon 94.[6]

The content of this record is limited to the names of the minister, the confirmed, parents and sponsors, and the date and place of administration. The minister is inscribed since he is the qualified witness to the sacramental conferring. The confirmed and their parents because the former are the subjects while the latter distinguish the recipients.[7] The Roman Ritual declares that the same procedure must be followed in the matter of parental inscription as is laid down in the case of baptism when there is question of the legitimacy of the child or no knowledge is had of its parentage.[8] The older Ritual, too, demanded a separate listing on different pages of the males and females.[9] The same may well be followed today. The obligation following upon the acceptances of sponsorship in the administration of this Sacrament demand the recording of the names of such as fulfill this function. Finally, the date and the place are verifying signs and make for an authentic and complete recording.[10]

The question of the transmission of notice concerning confirmation to the pastor of baptism has been discussed previously hence there remains only the situation wherein the proper pastor of the confirmed was not present at the ceremony, *e. g.*, his subjects were confirmed in another church. In such a case the onus of transmission to him of the prescribed information falls upon the minister of the Sacrament. Either personally or through another the information may be given, in writing or orally. The best mode of transmission will be the same as directed in the case of baptismal transmission, use of an authentic document.[11] In the same place Blat declares that the transference is to be made with diligence in accord with the legislator's use of the word *quamprimum*.[12]

[6] S. C. C., February 8, 1919—*A. A. S.*, XI (1919), 280 ss.
[7] Blat, *Commentarium*, III, n. 96.
[8] Title XII, cap. III, 508.
[9] *Rit. Roman. Pauli V*, p. 377.
[10] Blat, *Commentarium*, III, n. 96.
[11] S. C. de Sacr., July 4, 1921, ns. 1-5—*A. A. S.*, XIII (1921), 349.
[12] *Ibid.*

Article II

The Book of the Dead

Canon 1238. Expleta tumulatione, minister in libro defunctorum describat nomen et aetatem defuncti, nomen parentum vel conjugis, tempus mortis, quis et quae Sacramenta ministraverit, locum et tempus tumulationis.

This, the fourth register of the parochial group, has had very little significance in the historical evolution of the parish registers.[13] It is reasonable to suppose that some cause must exist for the unchanging maintenance of the same definite constitution of this book. The reason may be found in the nature of its contents, which has been responsible for a virtual ignoring of the register of the deceased by canonical commentators. The fulfilling of the prescriptions of the law when applied to practical cases gives rise to no problems of great import hence the usual procedure of quoting Canon 1238 is employed by most authors.

Before taking up the discussion concerning those things to be entered in this book in accord with Canon 1238, it must be called to mind that the sick-call register cannot be employed as a source of information from which to draw a certificate of death. It is not, first of all, extensive enough in its content and then the register of the dead alone is able to bear the proper testimony concerning the death of a person.[14] Nor may any other source be utilized in drawing up a certificate, not only for this book but when it is a question of any of the records.[15]

The first concern of the above quoted Canon is with the time of registration. After the interment the record should be made it declares.[16] The time limit for this inscription can well be set as the same had in this question for the other books. The exclusion of negligence and the proximate possibility of foregoing the inscription will

[13] Chapter III, IV, No. 4.

[14] Giraldi, *Animad. et Addiment. ad Barbosam, "De officio et Potestate Parochi,"* I, 7, p. 63, n. 11.

[15] S. C. C., July 3, 1909, n. 2—*A. A. S.*, I (1909), 658.

[16] Canon 1238.

sufficiently define the matter.[17] The onus of this inscription is placed by the Code upon the minister, however this does not go contrary to the usual regulations concerning inscription since ordinarily and canonically the pastor will be the minister in the case.[18] Should it happen that another performs the ceremonies the pastor whose duty it is primarily to keep the parish registers is responsible for the inscription.[19] Hence if the minister or another makes the entries it remains for the pastor to subsign the same to constitute it an authentic document.[20]

The name of the person, baptismal and family name,[21] the age of the deceased (either by noting the date of birth or in definite numbers, if possible),[22] the names of parents or spouse as the circumstances demand, all these are to be incorporated in the record together with the former place of residence of the deceased.[23] In case the deceased was married more than once the name of the last consort is entered.[24]

The time of the death, *i. e.*, the precise date, day, month and year of demise,[25] and the cause [26] are next recorded. Following this, the spiritual status of the deceased is indicated by registering what Sacraments (Penance, Viaticum, Extreme Unction) were received before death and the name of the ministrant.[27] If the Sacraments were not administered then the reason, if any, for the omission is given.[28] The final entries concern the place and date of the sepulture, note being made of the church and the cemetery of the performance,[29] even though the burial was not from the parish church.[30]

[17] Blat, *Commentarium*, III, n. 506; Augustine, *A Commentary*, V, 312.

[18] Canon 462.

[19] Rossi, *La "Sepultura Ecclesiastica,"* n. 104.

[20] Vermeersch-Creusen, *Epitome*, II, n. 55.

[21] *Rit. Roman.*, XII, I, 506; Rossi, *op cit.*, n. 103, 1.

[22] The Roman Ritual favors the latter: XII, V, p. 512.

[23] *Rit. Roman.*, XII, V, p. 512.

[24] Rossi, *La "Sepultura Ecclesiastica,"* n. 103, 3.

[25] Rossi, *op. cit.*, n. 103, 4.

[26] *Fanfani, De Jure Parochorum*, p. 435.

[27] Rossi, *op cit.*, n. 103, 5.

[28] Fanfani, *De Jure Parochorum*, p. 435.

[29] Rossi, *La "Sepultura Ecclesiastica,"* n. 103, 6.

[30] *Rit. Roman. Pauli V*, p. 383.

Article III

The Register of the "Status Animarum"

Canon 470, § 1. Habeat parochus libros paroeciales . . . etiam librum de statu animarum accurate conficere pro viribus curet. . . .

Concerning this register alone of the five parochial books, the Code speaks in a purely relative manner. The record of the families in a parish is to be maintained, as well as the pastor is able to do so. No other Canon, after the fashion of the legislation on the registration of baptism, marriage, etc., can be found in the Code to serve as a complement or a more defining regulation to the prescription had in Canon 470, § 1. All in all, this register is a peculiar one by nature as well as in its undetermined regulation in comparison with the rather detailed legislation had for the other parochial books.[81]

Such a record is useful only in the proper parish where it is kept, hence the annual reporting concerning the parochial books, is not, by express legislation,[82] to include this parochial record. Its purpose, too, is of no great legal importance, rather it is the source of more or less ordinary information concerning the spiritual and physical constitution of the parish.[83]

The Roman Ritual contains the prescriptions, which the Code foregoes, for the proper keeping of this register.[84] The members of the parish are grouped according to families for registration. A definite amount of space, perhaps a page, depending on the size of the family, is reserved for the required information.[85] In this space will be indicated the names of the comprising members, the place of residence and other details of personal identification.[86] Then are added such notes as serve to demonstrate the spiritual status.[87]

[81] Fanfani, *De Jure Parochorum,* n. 83, Pruemmer, *Manuale,* p. 215.

[82] Canon 470, § 3.

[83] The Council of Trent, though not explicitly legislating for this book aptly phrased its purpose, *"Melius agnoscere oves,"* ss. XXIII, *de ref.* c. 1.

[84] XII, VI, 513.

[85] Mothon, *Institutions Canoniques,* I, n. 973.

[86] *Rit. Roman., ibid.*

[87] De Meester, *Juris Canonici,* I, II, n. 859, I; Fanfani, *De Jure Parochorum,* n. 83.

Personal identification is secured by entering the names and surnames, the professions and the domicile of the father and mother, master or mistress of the house.[38] Other members of the household, children and other relatives together with employees are indicated in like manner.[39] This last however is generally not practical in this country since employees ordinarily live in their own homes. Each person is given consideration in a special paragraph in which is recorded, beside the above mentioned information, the age and spiritual condition, particular notice being paid to the reception of the Sacraments.[40]

The Roman Ritual proposes the use of various signs to indicate the reception of the Sacraments.[41] In earlier Rituals, as that of Paul V, quite an extensive system was had, today, however, the minimum is employed. "B" affixed to the name of a person indicates Baptism has been received. "C" shows that the individual has made the First Holy Communion, while "Chr." demonstrates the fact that Confirmation has been received.[42] Some space should be left between the various names in case there be need in the future to indicate a change of residence or the decease of the person.[43]

Nothing further has a place in this register and private information particularly is to be kept out of this official parochial record. If certain circumstances exist which affect families or members of families of the parish which a future pastor should know, said information must be given him orally or through other channels when necessary, not through this book.

The census-taking or visitation of the parish [44] is the means to be used in securing such information as belongs in the fifth parochial book. This can be accomplished with a minimum of effort if prior to the actual visitation envelopes devised to obtain the necessary in-

[38] Mothon, *op. cit.*, n. 973, 1.

[39] *Rit. Roman.*, *ibid.*

[40] De Meester, *op. cit.*, I, II, n. 859.

[41] Pp. 512-513.

[42] *Rit. Roman.*, *ibid.*; Mothon, *Institutions Canoniques*, I, n. 973.

[43] Mothon, *ibid.*

[44] Fanfani, *De Jure Parochorum*, n. 83; De Meester, *Juris Canonici*, I, II, n. 859.

formation are sent to known parishioners for filling in. The questions are placed on the outside, leaving the interior for the contribution to the block collection. Such a procedure helps to make not only the visitation of the parish more complete but aids greatly in the case of each family.

The information obtained during the census-taking can then be transferred to the record of the *status animarum*. Another method is in vogue also, that of using index cards. Properly utilized no transcription is necessary and particularly in parishes of large transient population this method is very fine, since corrections are more easily made in this method. New cards can be readily made to replace old and out-moded ones.[45]

[45] Fanfani, *De Jure Parochorum*, n. 83; Vromant, *Jus Missionariorum*, II, n. 346, 1, 3.

APPENDIX

PRACTICAL SUGGESTIONS FOR THE INSCRIPTION OF THE REGISTERS

INSTEAD of forms for the registers and the certificates it is felt that properly grouped suggestions, based upon the commentary offered in this work, will prove of greater practical use. The reason is that unless very involved procedure were followed the samples inserted would on account of their brevity leave too much to the reader. Virtually all of the matter discussed here may be found scattered throughout the work but it is repeated here so that one may profit from the closer association of kindred points.

1. *General Suggestions*

Two types of registers, varying widely in their format, are in use today. The one is made up of a number of columns while the other takes the form of certificates bound in book form, as it were. The former appears to be the better not only from the viewpoint of inscription but also in consideration of its use as a reference book. It is conducive to a more clear-cut inscription and is better adapted for the registration of the out of the ordinary case. As a reference work it is much more convenient particularly when one is searching for a record concerning which rather indefinite information is had.

The book of this type is generally not without its failings, however. Neither is the form of the register nor its size at fault, but the desire to include as many places for inscriptions as possible hampers its usefulness. The too restricted size of the individual columns induces the use of abbreviations and otherwise cramped inscription. If a more generous column were made, though the life of the register for inscriptions would be somewhat shortened, it would be a first class aid to the elimination of labored and sometimes almost illegible records. In particular, the final column, that dedicated to remarks or observations, would be greatly benefited by such an enlargement, since in the baptismal and matrimonial registers this column may be subjected to many varied inscriptions. Finally, the record should cover the double page with a single number for the two pages and the individual records ought to be numbered for the current year.

The omission of one or more of the columns is another fault sometimes encountered. For instance, the baptismal register, the principal parochial book, is to be very extensive in content since it may possibly be required to bear several annotations at later dates, yet often it is found that there is no place for these additions. Also the arrangement of the columns in this book as well as in the others should be considered so that the continuity of the baptismal inscription is not broken up by the column for the annotations. Finally, it might be added in this connection that if temporary pad-forms are employed, a practise generally frowned upon unless the registers are permanently kept in a place distant from the scene of the administration of the Sacraments, the same order for inscription should be followed on these pads as is found in the register, else names, etc., may easily be confused.

2. *Inscription of the Baptismal Register*

The child's name, the names of the parents, the date of the baptism, the names of the sponsors and the minister, and the pastor's signature, if necessary, form the backbone of this record. The address of the parents identify them with the parish which may be of aid in a later search for the record. The place and date of birth are helpful particularly in the search for unindexed records later and in general when incompletely informed persons are seeking the certificates because they remember the date of birth always but usually forget the date of baptism.

Concerning the annotations it must be admitted that difficulty is encountered when one attempts a symmetrical arrangement for their inclusion without rendering the register a book of huge size. The employment of one large column seems to recommend itself as the best procedure. The uppermost part of this column can be used for the annotation of Confirmation and because of the brevity of this addition it can be written across the width of the column, giving merely the date and the place of the administration and the name of the minister. Save for a small space at the bottom the remainder of the column can be evenly divided lengthwise. On one side of the dividing line will be the spaces for the annotations of Holy Orders and religious profession. These, too, are rather brief, the former being comprised of the date, the place and the name of the minister of the Sacrament while the latter will consist of the date, the place (religious order and abbey, for instance) and the name of him who received the profession. The other side will be dedicated to the matrimonial annotation giving the names of the other party to the marriage and the witnesses. Then the place of celebration and the name of the officiant.[1] The remaining space at the bottom which covers the width of the column is meant for the inscription of the nullity of the marriage, dispensation from Orders, etc.

The final column of the baptismal register as has been said before should also be of considerable size, larger than is usually found. This is the space given over to remarks. After considering the amount of information that might possibly need insertion here, it is estimated that the average size should amount to that sufficient to care for at least three of such insertions.

First of all it may be necessary to indicate the fact that the parents of the child are not married. This is not to be done by the use of the abbreviation, *fil. illegit.*, as has been explained in the commentary, but rather an indirect method is chosen. The illegitimacy is readily apparent if one or the other or both parents' names are missing from the register, hence no need of any indicative mark. In case that both parents' names are entered yet the child is not legitimate, the remarks' column should carry an inscription such as *extra matr. natus* or *ex matr. civili.* In these same cases where one or both parents' names are entered though the child is illegitimate the reason why their names are included must be noted together with reference to any documents had in support of these reasons.

[1] Today it might not be impractical to give consideration to the idea of a second marriage by one of the parties. In most cases this could be cared for by using the other side of the column since a twice married individual will scarcely ever need the Holy Order and religious profession spaces. Canon 984, 4°.

The point on the inscription of the illegitimate child is another good reason for not employing the usual brand of certificate register since many times its formation presumes that all children born are legitimate, hence from time to time it will be necessary to strike out the word legitimate thereby giving a certain clue to the illegitimacy. Also, the other possibilities given above in cases of illegitimacy are not easily cared for by this type of register.

Notations concerning conditional baptism, private baptism and the supplying of the ceremonies at baptism, paying close attention to the matter of the impediment of spiritual relationship, that is, expressly indicating when it so happens that the impediment is not contracted, must be considered. These things complete the list of possibilities that may need to be entered in the column of remarks.

In general baptismal certificates conform rather well with the necessities of the matter. However, seldom does one find in them a space dedicated to the inscription of the annotations that appear in the register itself and should sometimes be added to the certificate. Usually the lower left hand side of the certificate is quite blank hence they could very well be placed there.

There are some types of what might be called skeleton certificates on the market which permit the entrance of the name of the child, the parents and the minister, together with the date of birth and baptism. They omit the sponsors' names, forgetting the impediment of spiritual relationship, the annotations and the date of issue. This last, as well, is important since a certificate of any age may be a very potent instrument of fraud.

3. *Inscription of the Matrimonial Register*

This is another register that requires some special attention. The proper order of this record will be best observed by arranging the columns thus: the names of the parties, with the street address and parish, their respective ages, the names of the parents, witnesses' names and parishes, date and place of the marriage, name of the officiant and finally the column of remarks.

Other than the two final columns these matters do not require any specific attention. The column for the officiant's name however is the subject of one practical suggestion which at the same time may be applied to the other registers as well. It should be sufficient in extent to admit of the pastor's signature as well in cases where a delegate performs the ceremony. Incidentally the fact that he is a delegate should be noted in the register immediately after his signature or name, particularly if he has been delegated for this individual marriage.

It is the column of remarks that must bear the brunt of the possible additional inscriptions in the matrimonial registers. Dispensations, their kind and the chancery number with a note as to where they may be found, are recorded herein. Permission of the proper pastor for the performance of the ceremony should likewise be inscribed. Convalidations, decrees of nullity, use of the Pauline Privilege, conditions attached to a marriage, all these things are possible additions to a marriage record and should be recorded in the column of remarks when and if they occur. It is unreasonable to expect the column of the remarks to be of such a size that it could care for all of these things in the one marriage, however, it might not be too fanciful to suggest that space be made for the inclusion of at least three of these same. The number of the civil license may well be included particularly if it is one from another county.

The certificate of marriage is generally well-drawn but often fails to include the date of issuance and the observation that the marriage was performed in accord with the laws of the State on marriage. While concerned with the matter of the marriage certificate it would be of value to say a few words about the certificate of notification of marriage.

There is a custom in some places of reversing the baptismal certificate which has been obtained for the marriage and inscribing the notification of the marriage on its back, adding of course the pastoral signature and the parochial seal. Now this is a procedure that can easily become dangerous since one may unconsciously get into the habit of reporting only part of the required information to the pastor of baptism. Accordingly a special blank should be employed, one divided into two parts for about three-fourths of the length of the blank. One side of this division is inscribed with the name of the groom, the date of his birth and baptism together, and the names of his father, mother and the male witness to the marriage. The other side of the division will contain the bride's name, the date of her birth and baptism together, the names of her father and mother, and the name of the female witness. Below these things and outside the division, the certification is made that the marriage was performed according to the rites of the Church and the laws of the State with the date of the performance. Finally the signature of the pastor and the parochial seal are added.

4. *Inscription of the Register of the Confirmed*

The best form for these inscriptions is to have the certification at the top of the page which certification declares that Confirmation was conferred, with the minister's name, the church of administration, its location (city or town), and the date. Then one of the double pages is used for the entry of the boys and the other for the girls. Three columns will be necessary. The first for the names, baptismal and confirmational, as well as the last name, the second for the parents' names and the third for the name of the sponsor. The rules that govern legitimacy for the baptismal inscription must be employed here also when such a question is moved for parental inscription. The final inscription to be made to the register will be the signature of the pastor placed at the end of the list of the confirmed.

The certificate of confirmation may be made up in a special form or the letter form utilized. It should contain names of the child, parents, sponsor and the minister, together with the name of the church, the location and the date. Finally, it must be signed by the pastor and impressed with the parochial seal. A properly annotated baptismal certificate would serve the same purpose, since it would include the fact of confirmation.

5. *Inscription of the Register of the Dead*

This register presents no practical difficulties. The columns will be well arranged in this order: The names of the deceased, his parents or spouse (the latest consort), the date of birth and death in one column, the Sacraments administered in one column, the minister's name and the place and date of burial. The certificate will likewise include all of this with the pastor's signature, parochial seal and the date of issuance added.

6. *Inscription of the Register of the "Status Animarum"*

The arrangement of this register depends upon the pastor's ability to collect information concerning his people and hence it must be regulated as he is able to do so. The possibilities of this registration as set forth in the final chapter of the commentary [2] carry the full consideration of the matter to which nothing can be added here. Finally, there is no certificate to be issued drawn from this register, save for the notification by the former pastor sent to the new pastor in the case of a family changing parishes.

[2] Chapter VI, pp. 82-84.

BIBLIOGRAPHY

Sources

Acta Apostolicae Sedis (*A. A. S.*), Romae, 1909.

Acta et Decreta Concilii Plenarii Baltimorensis, I and II, Baltimore, 1868.

Acta et Decreta Sacrorum Conciliorum Recentiorum, 7 vols. (*Collectio Lacensis*), Friburgi-Brisgoviae, 1876.

Acta Ecclesiae Mediolanensis, 2 tomes, new edition, Ludguni, 1682 (A. E. M.).

Acta Sanctae Sedis (*A. S. S.*), 41 vols., Romae, 1865-1908.

Bullarium Diplomatum et Privilegiorum Sanctorum Romanorum Pontificium, 24 vols., Augustae-Taurinorum, 1857.

Codex Juris Canonici, Romae, 1918.

Codicis Juris Canonici Fontes, 5 vols., Romae, 1923-1930.

Collectanea Sacrae Congregationis de Propaganda Fide, 2 vols., Romae, 1907.

Corpus Juris Civilis (*Novellae Justiniani*), 3 vols., Schoell-Kroll, Berolini, 1928.

Harduin, J., *Conciliorum Collectio Regis Maxima*, 12 vols., Parisiis, 1715.

Hartzheim, J., *Concilia Germaniae quae . . . J. F. Schannat magna exorte primum collegit*, 11 vols., Cologne, 1759-1790.

Mansi, J., *Sacrorum Conciliorum Nova et Amplissima Collectio*, 51 vols., Parisiis, 1901-1927.

Rituale Romanum Pauli V Pont. Max Jussu Editum, Antverpiae, 1744.

Rituale Romanum Pii Papae XI ad Normam Codicis Juris Canonici Accomodatum, Romae, 1928.

References

Ayrinhac, H., *Marriage Legislation in the New Code of Canon Law*, New York, 1918.

——— *Penal Legislation*, New York, 1920.

[Bachofen], C. Augustine, *A Commentary on the New Code of Canon Law*, 8 vols., St. Louis, 1922.

Baruffaldus, J., *Ad Rituale Romanum Commentaria*, 2 vols., Florentiae, 1847.

Bastnagel, C., *Appointment of Parochial Adjutants and Assistants*, Washington, 1930.

Bernardus Papiensis, *Summa Decretalium*, ed. Laspeyres, Ratisbonae, 1860.

Bingham, J., *The Antiquities of the Christian Church*, 2 vols., London, 1856.

Blat, A., *Commentarium Textus Codicis Juris Canonici*, 5 vols., Romae, 1921-1927.

Bona, J., *Rerum Liturgicarum*, 3 vols., Taurinensis, 1747-1753.

Bouix, *Tractatus de Parocho*, Parisiis, 1855.

Bouuaert-Simeon, *Manuale Juris Canonici*, 3 ed., Gandae-Leodii, 1930.

Cabrol-Leclercq, *Dictionnaire D'Archeologie Chretienne et De Liturgie,* 20 vols., Parisiis, 1924.

Cappello, F., *Tractatus Canonico—Moralis De Sacramentis,* 2. ed., 3 vols., Taurinorum-Augustae, 1928.

Catalanus, J., *Rituale Romanum Benedicti Papae XIV Jussu Editum et Auctum, Perpetuis Commentariis Exornatum,* 2 tomes, Patavii, 1760.

Catholic Encyclopedia, The., 17 vols., New York, 1907-1922.

Chelodi, J., *Jus De Personis, Tridenti,* 1927.

Cocchi, G., *Commentarium in Codicem Juris Canonici,* 2. and 3. ed., 8 vols., Taurinorum-Augustae, 1925-1930.

D'Annibale, I., *Summula Theologiae Moralis,* 3 vols., Romae, 1908.

De Meester, A., *Compendium Juris Canonici et Juris Canonico-Civilis,* new edition, Bruges, 1921.

Denziger-Baanwart, *Enchiridion Symbolorum, Definitionum et Declarationum,* 14. and 15. ed., Friburgi-Brisgoviae, 1922.

Devoti, J., *Institutionum Canonicarum Libri IV,* Leodii, 1860.

Elliott, B. K. and Wm., *A Treatise on the Law of Evidence,* Vol. I (*General Principles*), Indianapolis, 1904.

Esmein, A., *Le Mariage en Droit Canonique,* 2 vols., Parisiis, 1891.

Fanfani, L., *De Jure Parochorum,* Taurini-Romae, 1924.

Ferraris, L., *Prompta Bibliotheca Canonica,* Parisiis, 1865.

Funk, F., *A Manual of Church History,* 2 vols. (4th impression of authorized translation from 5th German edition), St. Louis, 1910.

Gasparri, P., *Tractatus Canonicus De Matrimonio,* 3. ed. (1904), new edition (1932), 2 vols. Parisiis.

Genicot-Salsmans, *Institutiones Theologia Moralis,* 11 ed., 2 vols., Bruxellis, 1927.

Giraldi, U., *Animadversiones et Addimenta ad Barbosam "De officio et potestate Parochi,"* Romae, 1744.

Heiner-Wynen, *De Processu Criminali Ecclesiastico,* Romae, 1912.

Hostiensis (Henricus De Segusio), *Commentaria in V Libros Decretalium,* 3 vols., Venetiis, 1581.

Mabillion, J., *Praefationes in Acta Sanctarum Ordinis S. Benedicti in Classes Saeculorum Distributa,* 9 vols., Venetiis, 1783.

Migne, J., *Patrologiae Cursus Completus, Series Graeca,* 161 vols., Parisiis, 1858-1864 (*M. P. G.*).

———, *Patrologiae Cursus Completus, Series Latina,* 221 vols., Parisiis, 1844-1855 (*M. P. L.*).

Monacelli, F., *Formularium Fori Ecclesiastici,* 3. ed., 2 vols., Romae, 1894.

Montault, X., *Construction L'Ameublement Decoration Des Eglises,* 2 vols., Parisiis, 1885.

Mothon, J., *Institutions Canoniques,* 3 vols., Parisiis, 1922.

Munerati, *Elementa Juris Ecclesiastici, Romae,* 1926.

Pallavicino, S., *Istoria del Concilio di Trento,* 4 vols., Romae, 1833.

Panormitanus (Nicholas de Tudeschis), *Commentaria in Quinque Libros Decretalium,* 8 vols., Venetiis, 1578.

Payen, G., *De Matrimonio in Missionibus ac Potissimum in Sinis Tractatus et Casus,* 3 vols., Zikawei, 1928-1929.

Pruemmer, D., *Manuale Juris Canonici,* 4. and 5. ed., Friburgi-Brisgoviae, 1927.

Rittershuttius, C., *Expositio Methodica Novellarum Imperatoris Justiniani,* 2. ed., Florentiae, 1839.

Rossi, J., *De Paroecia,* Romae, 1923.

Rossi, J., La "Sepultura Ecclesiastica" e L "Jus Funerum," Bergamo, 1920.

Saegmüller, "Die Entstchung und Entwicklung der Kirchenbücher im Katholischen Deutschland bis zur Mitte der 18 Jahrhunderts"—*Theologische Quartalschrift,* vol. 81 (1899). (*T. Q. S.*).

Sanchez, T., *De Sancto Matrimonii Sacramento Disputationum,* 3 tomes, Lugduni, 1669.

Schmalzgrueber, F., *Jus Ecclesiasticum Universum,* 12 vols., Romae, 1844.

Şelvagio, J., *Antiquitatum Christianarum Institutiones,* 6 vols., Venetiis, 1794.

Sherman, *Roman Law in the Modern World,* 2. ed., 2 vols., New York, 1924.

Sipos, S., *Enchiridion Juris Canonici,* Pecs, 1926.

Smith, S., *Elements of Ecclesiastical Law,* 4. ed., New York, 1881.

Smith & Cheetham, *A Dictionary of Christian Antiquities,* 2 vols., Hartford, 1880.

Tanquerey, A., *Synopsis Theologiae Dogmaticae,* 21. ed., 3 vols., Romae, 1929.

Thomassinus, L., *Vetus et Nova Ecclesiae Disciplina,* 10 vols., Magonatiaci, 1787.

Van Espen, Z., *Jus Ecclesiasticum Universum Ceteraque Scripta Omnia,* Venetiis, 1769.

Veermersch-Creusen, *Epitome Juris Canonici,* 4. ed., 3 vols., Mechliniae-Romae, 1929.

Vering, *Bibliotheque Theologique du XIX Siecle,* vol. 1 (Droit Canon), Parisiis, 1879.

Villien, *A History of the Commandments of the Church,* St. Louis, 1915.

Vlaming, Th. M., *Praelectiones Juris Matrimonii,* 3. ed., 2 vols., Bussum in Hollandia, 1921.

Vromant, G., *Jus Missionariorum* (vol. II, *De Personis*), Lovanii, 1928.

Wernz-Vidal, *Jus Canonicum,* 2. ed., 5 vols., Romae, 1928.

Wigmore, J. H., *A Treatise on the Anglo-American System of Evidence in Trials at Common Law,* 2. ed., 5 vols., Boston, 1923.

Wouters, L., *De Forma Promissionis et Celebrationis Matrimonii,* 5. ed., Bussum in Hollandia, 1919.

Zollmann, C., *American Church Law,* St. Paul, 1933.

PERIODICALS

Il Monitore Ecclesiastico, Romae, 1888.—

Nouvelle Revue Theologique, Parisiis, 1856.—(*N. R. T.*).

Theologische Quartalschrift, Ravensburg, 1818.—(*T. Q. S.*).

Universitas Catholica Americae

WASHINGTON, D. C.

Facultas Juris Canonici

No. 88

1934

ALPHABETICAL INDEX

BIOGRAPHICAL NOTE

James John O'Rourke was born in Philadelphia, December 22, 1905, and educated in St. Patrick's Parochial School and the Roman Catholic High School for Boys in that city. His philosophical and theological studies were made at St. Charles Seminary, Overbrook, Philadelphia, after which he entered the School of Canon Law at the Catholic University of America, in 1931. From this institution he received his Bachelor and Licentiate Degrees in 1931-32. He was ordained to the priesthood on May 21, 1932, by His Eminence, D. Cardinal Dougherty, Archbishop of Philadelphia.

CANON LAW STUDIES

1. FRERIKS, REV. CELESTINE A., C.PP.S., J.C.D., Religious Congregations in Their External Relations, 121 pp., 1916.
2. GALLIHER, REV. DANIEL M., O.P., J.C.D., Canonical Elections, 117 pp., 1917.
3. BORKOWSKI, REV. AURELIUS L., O.F.M., De Confraternitatibus Ecclesiasticis, 136 pp., 1918.
4. CASTILLO, REV. CAYO, J.C.D., Disertacion Historico-canonica sobre la Potestad del Cabildo en Sede Vacante o Impedida del Vicario Capitular, 99 pp., 1919 (1918).
5. KUBELBECK, REV. WILLIAM J., S.T.B., J.C.D., The Sacred Penitentiaria and Its Relations to Faculties of Ordinaries and Priests, 129 pp., 1918.
6. PETROVITS, REV. JOSEPH J. C., S.T.D., J.C.D., The New Church Law on Matrimony, X-461 pp., 1919.
7. HICKEY, REV. JOHN J., S.T.B., J.C.D., Irregularities and Simple Impediments in the New Code of Canon Law, 100 pp., 1920.
8. KLEKOTKA, REV. PETER J., S.T.B., J.C.D., Diocesan Consultors, 179 pp., 1920.
9. WANNENMACHER, REV. FRANCIS, J.C.D., The Evidence in Ecclesiastical Procedure Affecting the Marriage Bond, 1920. (Not Printed.)
10. GOLDEN, REV. HENRY FRANCIS, J.C.D., Parochial Benefices in the New Code, IV-119 pp., 1921. (Printed 1925.)
11. KOUDELKA, REV. CHARLES, J., J.C.D., Pastors, Their Rights and Duties According to the New Code of Canon Law, 211 pp., 1921.
12. MELO, REV. ANTONIUS, O.F.M., J.C.D., De Exemptione Regularium, X-188 pp., 1921.
13. SCHAAF, REV. VALENTINE THEODORE, O.F.M., S.T.B., J.C.D., The Cloister, X-180 pp., 1921.
14. BURKE, REV. THOMAS JOSEPH, S.T.B., J.C.D., Competence in Ecclesiastical Tribunals, IV-117 pp., 1922.
15. LEECH, REV. GEORGE LEO, J.C.D., A Comparative Study of the Constitution "Apostolicae Sedis" and the "Codex Juris Canonici," 179 pp., 1922.
16. MOTRY, REV. HUBERT LOUIS, S.T.D., J.C.D., Diocesan Faculties According to the Code of Canon Law, II-167 pp., 1922.
17. MURPHY, REV. GEORGE LAWRENCE, J.C.D., Delinquencies and Penalties in the Administration and the Reception of the Sacraments, IV-121 pp., 1923.
18. O'REILLY, REV. JOHN ANTHONY, S.T.B., J.C.D., Ecclesiastical Sepulture in the New Code of Canon Law, II-129 pp., 1923.
19. MICHALICKA, REV. WENCESLAS CYRILL, O.S.B., J.C.D., Judicial Procedure in Dismissal of Clerical Exempt Religious, 107 pp., 1923.

20. Dargin, Rev. Edward Vincent, S.T.B., J.C.D., Reserved Cases According to the Code of Canon Law, IV-103 pp., 1924.
21. Godfrey, Rev. John A., S.T.B., J.C.D., The Right of Patronage According to the Code of Canon Law, 153 pp., 1924.
22 Hagedorn, Rev. Francis Edward, J.C.D., General Legislation on Indulgences, II-154 pp., 1924.
23. King, Rev. James Ignatius, J.C.D., The Administration of the Sacraments to Dying Non-Catholics, V-141 pp., 1924.
24. Winslow, Rev. Francis Joseph, A.F.M., J.C.D., Vicars and Prefects Apostolic, IV-149 pp., 1924.
25. Correa, Rev. Jose Servelion, S.T.L., J.C.D., La Potestad Legislativa de la Iglesia Católica, IV-127 pp., 1925.
26. Dugan, Rev. Henry Francis, M.A., J.C.D., The Judiciary Department of the Diocesan Curia, 87 pp., 1925.
27. Keller, Rev. Charles Frederick, S.T.B., J.C.D., Mass Stipends, 167 pp., 1925.
28. Paschang, Rev. John Linus, J.C.D., The Sacramentals According to the Code of Canon Law, 129 pp., 1925.
29. Piontek, Rev. Cyrillus, O.F.M., S.T.B., J.C.D., De Indulto Exclaustrationis necnon Saecularizationis, XIII-289 pp., 1925.
30. Kearney, Rev. Richard Joseph, S.T.B., J.C.D., Sponsors at Baptism According to the Code of Canon Law, IV-127 pp., 1925.
31. Bartlett, Rev. Chester Joseph, A.M., LL.B., J.C.D., The Tenure of Parochial Property in the United States of America, V-108 pp., 1926.
32. Kilker, Rev. Adrian Jerome, J.C.D., Extreme Unction, V-425 pp. 1926.
33. McCormick, Rev. Robert Emmett, J.C.D., Confessors of Religious, VIII-266 pp., 1926.
34. Miller, Rev. Newton Thomas, J.C.D., Founded Masses According to the Code of Canon Law, VII-93 pp., 1926.
35. Roelker, Rev. Edward G., S.T.D., J.C.D., Principles of Privilege According to the Code of Canon Law, XI-166 pp., 1926.
36. Bakalarczyk, Rev. Richardus, M.I.C., J.U.D., De Novitiatu, VIII-208 pp., 1927.
37. Pizzuti, Rev. Lawrence, O.F.M., J.U.L., De Parochis Religiosis, 1927. (Not Printed.)
38. Bliley, Rev. Nicholas Martin, O.S.B., J.C.D., Altars According to the Code of Canon Law, XIX-132 pp., 1927.
39. Brown, Brendan Francis, A.B., LL.M., J.U.D., The Canonical Juristic Personality with Special Reference to its Status in the United States of America, V-212 pp., 1927.
40. Cavanaugh, Rev. William Thomas, C.P., J.U.D., The Reservation of the Blessed Sacrament, VIII-101 pp., 1927.
41. Doheny, Rev. William J., C.S.C., A.B., J.U.D., Church Property: Modes of Acquisition, X-118 pp,. 1927

42. Feldhaus, Rev. Aloysius H., C.PP.S., J.C.D., Oratories, IX-141 pp., 1927.
43. Kelly, Rev. James Patrick, A.B., J.C.D., The Jurisdiction of the Simple Confessor, X-208 pp., 1927.
44. Neuberger, Rev. Nicholas J., J.C.D., Canon 6 or the Relation of the Codex Juris Canonici to the Preceding Legislation, V-95 pp., 1927.
45. O'Keeffe, Rev. Gerald Michael, J.C.D., Matrimonial Dispensations, Powers of Bishops, Priests, and Confessors, VIII-232 pp., 1927.
46. Quigley, Rev. Joseph, A.M., A.B., J.C.D., Condemned Societies, 139 pp., 1927.
47. Zaplotnik, Rev. Ioannes Leo, J.C.D., De Vicariis Foraneis, X-142 pp., 1927.
48. Duskie, Rev. John Aloysius, A.B., J.C.D., The Canonical Status of the Orientals in the United States, VIII-196 pp., 1928.
49. Hyland, Rev. Francis Edward, J.C.D., Excommunication, Its Nature, Historical Development and Effects, VIII-181 pp., 1928.
50. Reinmann, Rev. Gerald Joseph, O.M.C., J.C.D., The Third Order Secular of Saint Francis, 201 pp., 1928.
51. Schenk, Rev. Francis J., J.C.D., The Matrimonial Impediments of Mixed Religion and Disparity of Cult, XVI-318 pp., 1929.
52. Coady, Rev. John Joseph, S.T.D., J.U.D., A.M., The Appointment of Pastors, VIII-150 pp., 1929.
53. Kay, Rev. Thomas Henry, J.C.D., Competence in Matrimonial Procedure, VIII-164 pp., 1929.
54. Turner, Rev. Sidney Joseph, C.P., J.U.D., The Vow of Poverty, XLIX-217 pp., 1929.
55. Kearney, Rev. Raymond A., A.B., S.T.D., J.C.D., The Principles of Delegation, VII-149 pp., 1929.
56. Conran, Rev. Edward James, A.B., J.C.D., The Interdict, V-163 pp., 1930.
57. O'Neil, Rev. William H., J.C.D., Papal Rescripts of Favor, VII-218 pp., 1930.
58. Bastnagel, Rev. Clement Vincent, J.U.D., The Appointment of Parochial Adjutants and Assistants, XV-257 pp., 1930.
59. Ferry, Rev. William A., A.B., J.C.D., Stole Fees, X-107 pp., 1930.
60. Costello, Rev. John Michael, A.B., J.C.D., Domicile and Quasi-Domicile, VII-201 pp., 1930.
61. Kremer, Rev. Michael Nicholas, A.B., S.T.B., J.C.D., Church Support in the United States, VI-136 pp., 1930.
62. Angulo, Rev. Luis, C.M., J.C.D., Legislación de la Iglesia sobre la intención en la applicación de la Santa Misa, VII-104 pp., 1931.
63. Frey, Rev. Wolfgang Norbert, O.S.B., A.B., J.C.D., The Act of Religious Profession, VIII-174 pp., 1931.
64. Roberts, Rev. James Brendan, A.B., J.C.D., The Banns of Marriage, XIV-140 pp., 1931.

65. Ryder, Rev. Raymond Aloysius, A.B., J.C.D., Simony, IX-151 pp., 1931.
66. Campagna, Rev. Angelo, Ph.D., J.U.D., Il Vicario Generale del Vescovo, VII-205 pp., 1931.
67. Cox, Rev. Joseph Godfrey, A.B., J.C.D., The Administration of Seminaries, VI-124 pp., 1931.
68. Gregory, Rev. Donald J., J.U.D., The Pauline Privilege, XV-165 pp., 1931.
60. Donohue, Rev. John F., J.C.D., The Impediment of Crime, VIII-110 pp., 1931.
70. Dooley, Rev. Eugene A., O.M.I., J.C.D., Church Law on Sacred Relics, IX-143 pp., 1931.
71. Orth, Rev. Clement Raymond, O.M.C., J.C.D., The Approbation of Religious Institutes, 171 pp., 1931.
72. Pernicone, Rev. Joseph M., A.B., J.C.D., The Ecclesiastical Prohibition of Books, XII-267 pp., 1932.
73. Clinton, Rev. Connell, A.B., J.C.D., The Paschal Precept, IX-108 pp., 1932.
74. Donnelly, Rev. Francis B., A.M., S.T.L., J.C.D., The Diocesan Synod, VIII-125 pp., 1932
75. Torrente, Rev. Camilo, C.M.F., J.C.D., Las Processiones Sagradas, V-145 pp., 1932.
76. Murphy, Rev. Edwin J., C.PP.S., J.C.D., Suspension Ex Informata Conscientia, XI-122 pp., 1932.
77. MacKenzie, Rev. Eric F., A.M., S.T.L., J.C.D., The Delict of Heresy in its Commission, Penalization, Absolution, VII-124 pp., 1932.
78. Lyons, Rev. Avitus E., S.T.B., J.C.D., The Collegiate Tribunal of First Instance, XI-147 pp., 1932.
79. Connolly, Rev. Thomas A., J.C.D., Appeals, XI-195 pp., 1932.
80. Sangmeister, Rev. Joseph V., A.B., J.C.D., Force and Fear as Precluding Matrimonial Consent, V-211 pp., 1932.
81. Jaeger, Rev. Leo A., A.B., J.C.D., The Administration of Vacant and Quasi-Vacant Episcopal Sees in the United States, IX-229 pp. 1932.
82. Rimlinger, Rev. Herbert T., J.C.D., Error Invalidating Matrimonial Consent, VII-79 pp., 1932.
83. Barrett, Rev. John D. M., S.S., J.C.D., Comparative Study of the Third Plenary Council and the Code, IX-221 pp., 1932.
84. Carberry, Rev. John J., Ph.D., S.T.D., J.C.L., The Juridical Form of Marriage, 1934.
85. Dolan, Rev. John L., A.B., J.C.L., The Defensor Vinculi, 1934.
86. Hannan, Rev. Jerome D., A.M., S.T.D., LL.B., J.C.L., The Cannon Law of Wills, 1934.
87. Lemieux, Rev. Lelisle A., A.M., J.C.L., The Sentence in Ecclesiastical Procedure, 1934.
88. O'Rourke, Rev. James J., A.B., J.C.L., Parish Registers, 1934.

89. TIMLIN, REV. BARTHOLOMEW, O.F.M., A.M., J.C.L., Conditional Matrimonial Consent, 1934.
90. WAHL, REV. FRANCIS X., A.B., J.C.L., The Matrimonial Impediments of Consanguinity and Affinity, 1934.
91. WHITE, REV. ROBERT J., A.B., LL.B., S.T.B., J.C.L., Canonical Ante-Nuptial Promises and the Civil Law, 1934.

www.ingramcontent.com/pod-product-compliance
Lightning Source LLC
LaVergne TN
LVHW050201080826
844660LV00012B/332

* 9 7 8 0 8 1 3 2 2 2 7 7 6 *